TABLE OF CONTENTS

Part I: Early Life and Influences 1
    Chapter 1: The Making of a Rebel: 1
    Chapter 2: A Life Interrupted: 7
    Chapter 3: The Artist and the Activist: 12
    Chapter 4: A Meeting of Minds and Hearts: 19

Part II: The Rise of a Visionary 26
    Chapter 5: Self-Portrait as a Revolution: 26
    Chapter 6: Pain and Beauty: The Symbolism of Suffering: 32
    Chapter 7: The Surrealist Embrace: 37
    Chapter 8: Mexico in Her Art: 43

Part III: Love, Loss, and Resilience 51
    Chapter 9: A Stormy Marriage: 51
    Chapter 10: The Power of Self-Expression: 56
    Chapter 11: Finding Strength in Pain: 62
    Chapter 12: Beyond the Physical: 69

Part IV: Legacy and Impact 77
    Chapter 13: The Rise of a Feminist Icon: 77
    Chapter 14: The Art of Frida Kahlo: 83
    Chapter 15: Frida Kahlo: A Global Icon: 92
    Chapter 16: The Frida Kahlo Museum: 98
    Chapter 17: Frida Kahlo's Continuing Influence: 104
    Chapter 18: The Enduring Legacy: 109

Part I: Early Life and Influences

Chapter 1: The Making of a Rebel:

Birth and childhood in Coyoacán, Mexico

Frida Kahlo, the iconic Mexican painter known for her self-portraits imbued with vibrant colors and surreal imagery, was born on July 6, 1907, in the heart of Coyoacán, a quaint and historic neighborhood in Mexico City. This vibrant and culturally rich neighborhood would leave an indelible mark on her art and her spirit, shaping her identity as a Mexican woman and an artist.

Her birth home, the Blue House, a modest yet charming dwelling painted in a vibrant shade of blue, became a symbol of her life and artistic legacy. This house, now a museum dedicated to her life and work, stands as a testament to her vibrant personality and artistic spirit. Coyoacán, known for its colonial architecture, lush gardens, and rich cultural heritage, served as a backdrop to Frida's formative years, exposing her to the beauty of Mexican traditions, folklore, and indigenous culture.

Her parents, Guillermo Kahlo, a German-born photographer, and Matilde Calderón y González, a Mexican homemaker, were both individuals of strong personalities and deep cultural roots. Guillermo, a passionate photographer who documented the beauty and the people of Mexico, instilled in his daughter an appreciation for the power of imagery and storytelling. Matilde, a woman of strength and resilience, played a crucial role in shaping Frida's independence and her unwavering spirit.

Frida's childhood was a tapestry woven with the vibrant threads of Mexican culture and tradition. She was exposed to the rich tapestry of indigenous art, folklore, and religious practices, elements that would later find their way into her paintings. Her parents encouraged her to engage in creative pursuits, fostering her early artistic talents. Even as a young child, Frida showed a natural inclination toward art, drawing and painting with remarkable passion and talent.

The vibrant and bustling atmosphere of Coyoacán, with its bustling markets, colorful houses, and vibrant street life, fostered in Frida a deep sense of connection to her Mexican heritage. The neighborhood's rich history, a blend of pre-Columbian, Spanish colonial, and indigenous influences, provided Frida with a unique perspective on Mexican identity and culture.

Her childhood, spent amidst the beauty and cultural richness of Coyoacán, was a crucial period in shaping her artistic vision. It was in these early years, surrounded by the vibrant tapestry of Mexican life, that Frida Kahlo began to develop the unique artistic voice that would later define her as a revolutionary artist and a powerful symbol of Mexican identity and female empowerment.

Early artistic inclinations and influences

Frida Kahlo's artistic journey began not with a paintbrush, but with a camera. Her father, Guillermo Kahlo, a renowned photographer, instilled in her a profound appreciation for capturing the world through a lens. This early exposure to photography, with its emphasis on capturing moments in time and revealing the nuances of light and shadow, would later inform her own artistic approach. In the family's studio, amidst the whirring of cameras and the scent of developing chemicals, Frida learned the technical aspects of photography, developing a keen eye for detail and composition. More importantly, she absorbed a deep-rooted understanding of the power of images to tell stories and evoke emotions.

However, Frida's artistic interests extended beyond the confines of the camera lens. She was captivated by the vibrant colors and intricate details of Mexican folk art, which was a prominent feature of her childhood environment. The rich tapestry of Mexican culture, with its deeply rooted indigenous traditions, resonated with Frida's spirit, nurturing a deep connection to her homeland and inspiring her own artistic exploration. She was particularly drawn to the expressive imagery of **retablos**, small devotional paintings depicting scenes of miracles and prayers, which showcased a stark, symbolic visual language that would later echo in her own art.

The influence of her mother, Matilde Calderón, cannot be ignored. While Matilde was a strong and independent woman, her influence on Frida's artistic inclinations was less direct but equally profound. Matilde's passion for *textiles* and *embroidery*, a craft deeply embedded in Mexican tradition, instilled in Frida a sense of color and pattern that would later inform her brushstrokes. Matilde's love for intricate details and her ability to weave together diverse elements into cohesive wholes, were traits that Frida would later emulate in her own art, creating canvases that were as intricate and captivating as the embroidered textiles she admired.

Frida's early life was immersed in a rich cultural melting pot, where she was exposed to diverse artistic influences.

These formative experiences – her father's photographic expertise, her mother's textile artistry, and the vibrant traditions of Mexican folk art – would profoundly shape her artistic sensibilities. These early influences would later converge in Frida's own unique artistic language, blending the technical precision of photography, the symbolic power of retablos, and the vibrant color and detail of Mexican textiles, creating a canvas where pain, passion, and identity were seamlessly interwoven.

The impact of her father, a photographer, and her mother's strong personality

Frida Kahlo's parents, Guillermo Kahlo and Matilde Calderón, played a significant role in shaping her artistic sensibility and personality. Her father, a **photographer** of German and Hungarian descent, instilled in her a keen eye for detail and a passion for capturing the essence of human emotion. He introduced her to the world of art and photography, taking her on photographic expeditions and teaching her the technical aspects of the craft. This early exposure to the visual arts undoubtedly ignited Frida's own creative impulses.

Frida's mother, Matilde Calderón, was a **strong-willed and independent woman** who embodied traditional Mexican values and beliefs. She was a devoted wife and mother, yet she possessed a fierce spirit and a unwavering determination. This indomitable spirit, coupled with her deep connection to Mexican culture, had a profound impact on Frida's worldview.

Frida's parents' relationship was a complex one, marked by both love and conflict. Her father's professional success contrasted with her mother's more domestic role, creating a dynamic that Frida would later explore in her art. Her parents' passionate love affair, punctuated by occasional arguments, exposed Frida to the complexities of human relationships, providing rich material for her later artistic explorations of love, pain, and loss.

The influence of her father's artistic sensibilities, combined with her mother's strong personality, created a unique blend of influences that would shape Frida Kahlo's life and art. Her father's photographic eye fostered her keen attention to detail and her ability to capture the raw emotion of a moment. Her mother's strength and resilience, along with her deep connection to Mexican culture, imbued Frida with a fierce independence and a profound sense of national identity. These influences, interwoven with her own personal experiences and struggles, would form the bedrock of her artistic vision, culminating in the creation of some of the most powerful and enduring images in the history of modern art.

Early encounters with Mexican culture and indigenous traditions

Frida Kahlo's early life was deeply intertwined with the vibrant tapestry of Mexican culture, a rich blend of indigenous heritage and colonial influences. Born in Coyoacán, a historic district of Mexico City, Kahlo was immersed in a world of vibrant colors, ancient traditions, and artistic expressions that would profoundly shape her worldview and artistic sensibilities. The neighborhood, once a pre-Hispanic village, preserved a palpable connection to the Aztec past, evident in its cobblestone streets, colonial architecture, and the enduring presence of indigenous crafts and rituals.

As a child, Kahlo was exposed to the rich heritage of Mexican folklore, a tradition passed down through generations of storytelling, music, and dance. Tales of mythical creatures, ancient gods, and heroic figures captivated her imagination, fueling a fascination with the supernatural and the power of symbolism. She witnessed the vibrant rituals and ceremonies of indigenous communities, where vibrant colors, elaborate costumes, and ancient rituals honored the cyclical nature of life and death. These early encounters sparked a lifelong fascination with the rich symbolism and powerful imagery that permeated Mexican culture.

Kahlo's home was a space where Mexican tradition and artistic expression intertwined. Her father, Guillermo Kahlo, a photographer of German descent, instilled in her a deep appreciation for visual beauty and the power of capturing moments in time. He was known for his meticulous documentation of Mexican folk art, architecture, and indigenous life, introducing his daughter to the beauty and complexity of her homeland. Her mother, Matilde Calderón, a devout Catholic, was a strong and independent woman who instilled in Kahlo a deep sense of family, tradition, and the importance of perseverance. She surrounded Frida with the warmth and tradition of Mexican home life, teaching her the art of cooking, sewing, and embroidery, skills that would later find their way into her artistic expression.

These early encounters with Mexican culture became foundational elements in Kahlo's artistic identity. She drew inspiration from the vibrant colors of indigenous textiles, the intricate designs of traditional pottery, and the symbolism embedded in ancient rituals. These influences would later find expression in her self-portraits, where she incorporated elements of pre-Hispanic art, folk imagery, and the raw power of Mexican folklore. The vibrant colors, bold patterns, and symbolic motifs that characterize her paintings were deeply rooted in the cultural landscape of her childhood, reflecting a profound connection to her heritage and a celebration of the enduring spirit of Mexico.

Kahlo's early encounters with Mexican culture and indigenous traditions were instrumental in shaping her worldview, her artistic sensibility, and her profound connection to her homeland. These experiences fostered a deep appreciation for the rich tapestry of her country's history, folklore, and artistic heritage, providing her with a reservoir of inspiration that would fuel her artistic revolution and make her a symbol of Mexican identity.

Chapter 2: A Life Interrupted:

The devastating bus accident and its lifelong consequences

On September 17, 1925, Frida Kahlo's life was irrevocably altered by a **devastating bus accident**. The collision, which involved a **streetcar** and a **bus** she was riding, left her with a **fractured spine**, a **broken collarbone**, a **fractured pelvis**, **dislocated right foot**, and **numerous other injuries**. The severity of her injuries was such that doctors initially doubted she would ever walk again.

The accident not only inflicted physical pain but also **deep emotional trauma**. The experience left Frida with a **constant sense of suffering**, a theme that would become central to her art. The accident also led to **years of physical pain and limitations**, forcing her to undergo **multiple surgeries and endure countless hours of rehabilitation**.

Despite the hardship, Frida's **spirit of resilience** remained unbroken. She used her art as a means to **confront her**

pain and **explore the complexities of her physical and emotional state**. The accident, rather than breaking her, served as a catalyst, pushing her to delve deeper into her own **inner world** and express her experiences through her art.

Frida's paintings often feature **stark imagery** depicting her physical wounds, medical equipment, and the **physical manifestations of her pain**. This raw and unflinching approach to her own suffering became a hallmark of her style, captivating audiences and establishing her as a **powerful voice for those who suffer**.

The accident's lasting impact on Frida's life is undeniable. It forced her to confront her own mortality and the fragility of the human body. It also shaped her perspective on life, leaving her with a **deep appreciation for the beauty and resilience of the human spirit**.

Despite the hardships she endured, Frida Kahlo's story is one of **unyielding determination** and **artistic triumph**. The accident, while deeply traumatic, became a driving force behind her art, pushing her to create a body of work that would **transform the landscape of art history** and inspire generations to come.

Early explorations of pain, suffering, and mortality in her art

The devastating bus accident that Frida Kahlo endured in 1925 was a pivotal moment in her life, not just for the physical injuries she sustained but also for the profound impact it had on her artistic sensibilities. This traumatic experience left her bedridden for months, her body wracked with pain and her spirit grappling with the fragility of life. This period marked the beginning of her intense exploration of themes of pain, suffering, and mortality in her art, themes that would come to define her unique artistic voice.

Even before the accident, Frida possessed a keen awareness of the transient nature of life. Growing up in Mexico City, she was exposed to the vibrant but often harsh realities of Mexican society, witnessing poverty, illness, and the inevitability of death. Her father, a photographer, instilled in her a deep appreciation for the beauty and fragility of the human form, while her mother, a strong and independent woman, taught her the importance of resilience and the power of the human spirit to overcome adversity.

After the accident, however, Frida's engagement with these themes deepened, becoming more personal and visceral. She began to translate her physical pain into artistic expressions, exploring the depths of human suffering with an unflinching honesty. Her early paintings, often self-portraits, became powerful visual narratives of her struggle to reclaim her body and spirit after the accident.

In *The Broken Column* (1944), for instance, Frida depicts herself standing upright, her body pierced by a large, broken column, symbolizing the physical and emotional pain that she endured. The image is stark and unsettling, yet there is a sense of defiance in Frida's pose, a determination to persevere despite her suffering. Similarly, in *Henry Ford Hospital* (1932), she portrays herself lying in a hospital bed, surrounded by medical instruments and symbols of her physical trauma. Her expression is one of intense pain and anguish, yet there is also a sense of vulnerability and surrender to her fate.

Frida's exploration of pain was not limited to her own experiences. She was deeply moved by the suffering of others, particularly those marginalized by society. Her paintings often depicted the human body as a site of both pain and resilience, a testament to the enduring spirit that can overcome even the most daunting challenges. In *Self-Portrait with Thorn Necklace and Hummingbird* (1940), Frida's face is contorted in pain, her neck adorned with a thorn necklace and a hummingbird hovering nearby. This image can be interpreted as a representation of the intertwined nature of love, pain, and death, a recurring theme in Frida's work.

Her exploration of mortality went beyond the physical realm. Frida was fascinated by the concept of death, viewing it not as an end but as a transformative process. She was drawn to the imagery of skulls, skeletons, and flowers, all symbols of the cyclical nature of life and death. In *The Two Fridas* (1939), she portrays two versions of herself, one with a severed artery connected to the other by a vascular system. This image suggests the interconnectedness of life and death, the two Fridas representing the duality of her own being.

Throughout her artistic career, Frida Kahlo remained fascinated by the human experience, especially the capacity for suffering and resilience. Her early explorations of pain, suffering, and mortality laid the foundation for her later works, which would delve deeper into themes of identity, womanhood, and the complexities of human relationships. Her art serves as a powerful testament to the enduring spirit of the human being, a reminder of the power of art to transform pain into beauty and vulnerability into strength.

The enduring impact of the accident on her physical and emotional well-being

The bus accident that Frida Kahlo suffered in 1925 was a defining moment in her life, shaping not only her physical existence but also her artistic vision and emotional landscape. The accident, a brutal collision that pinned her to a metal handrail, left her with a broken spine, a shattered pelvis, a broken collarbone, and numerous other injuries. The impact of the crash was profound, leaving her with chronic pain, physical limitations, and a deep psychological scar that would forever color her art.

The accident resulted in a series of surgical procedures that left her body permanently **marked** and **changed**. Throughout her life, she would endure multiple surgeries, hospitalizations, and bouts of debilitating pain. The accident's physical toll was a constant reminder of her vulnerability and mortality, a theme that would permeate her art.

Beyond the physical suffering, the accident had a profound impact on Frida's emotional well-being. The trauma of the crash, the physical limitations it imposed, and the constant pain she endured left her grappling with feelings of **isolation**, **vulnerability**, and **existential angst**. These emotions, combined with her already strong sense of **independence** and **rebellion**, fueled her artistic expression.

Her self-portraits, often characterized by unflinching honesty and a raw exploration of pain, became a powerful means of confronting her suffering and making sense of her fragmented reality. She used her art as a way to **process her trauma**, to **find meaning in her suffering**, and to **affirm her resilience** in the face of adversity.

The accident, while a devastating event, ultimately became a catalyst for Frida's artistic development. It forced her to confront the fragility of the human body, the power of

11

pain, and the impermanence of life. These themes, interwoven with her personal struggles, found expression in her art, making it a powerful and deeply personal reflection of her life's journey.

Frida Kahlo's art transcended the realm of mere autobiography. It became a universal language of pain, resilience, and the enduring human spirit. Her unflinching honesty about her suffering, coupled with her embrace of surrealism and symbolism, resonated with audiences across generations, making her a powerful icon for those who have experienced physical and emotional trauma.

Frida's art serves as a powerful reminder that pain can be a source of strength, that adversity can be transformed into art, and that the human spirit, even in the face of suffering, can find beauty, meaning, and resilience.

Chapter 3: The Artist and the Activist:

Early political awakening and her engagement with the Mexican Revolution

Frida Kahlo's life unfolded against the backdrop of a tumultuous era in Mexico. The Mexican Revolution, a period of intense social and political upheaval that spanned from 1910 to 1920, left an indelible mark on the nation's identity and artistic landscape. While Frida was born in 1907, after the revolution's initial phases, the echoes of this tumultuous period resonated deeply within the cultural fabric of her youth. She grew up in Coyoacán, a historic district of Mexico City, where the spirit of the revolution lingered in the air, shaping the conversations, beliefs, and artistic expressions of her time.

Her father, Guillermo Kahlo, was a passionate supporter of the revolution and a committed socialist. His political views were deeply ingrained in the family home, where Frida was exposed to discussions about social justice, equality, and the struggle against oppression. These ideas resonated with Frida's own burgeoning sense of rebellion and her desire for a more equitable world. Her father's unwavering commitment to leftist ideals planted the seeds of a strong political consciousness in Frida's young mind.

The revolution's impact was not confined to politics; it permeated Mexican art and culture. A new artistic movement, known as Mexican Muralism, emerged as a powerful force in expressing the revolution's ideals. Artists like Diego Rivera, José Clemente Orozco, and David Alfaro Siqueiros used murals to depict the revolution's struggles, its heroes, and its enduring spirit. These murals became powerful symbols of national pride and social change, inspiring a generation of artists and intellectuals.

Frida was drawn to the vibrant spirit of Mexican Muralism, which celebrated the indigenous heritage and cultural identity of Mexico. She witnessed firsthand the impact of these murals on the public consciousness, observing how they ignited conversations about social justice, political reform, and the nation's history. This exposure to the dynamic world of Mexican art fostered Frida's own artistic aspirations and fueled her desire to create work that would resonate with the complexities of her time.

However, Frida's political awakening went beyond the visual impact of murals. She was deeply influenced by the ideas of communism, which were gaining traction in Mexico during the post-revolutionary period. The communist movement promised a utopian society free from exploitation and inequality, appealing to Frida's innate sense of fairness and her desire for a better world. Her engagement with communist ideals was further amplified by her passionate relationship with Diego Rivera, a renowned muralist and staunch communist, whose influence on Frida's artistic and political views was profound.

Frida's early artistic experimentation reflected her growing political consciousness. Her paintings often incorporated themes of social justice, labor rights, and the struggles of the working class. She used her art to voice her concerns about the injustices she witnessed in Mexican society, embracing the revolutionary spirit that permeated the nation's artistic landscape. This early period marked the beginning of a lifelong engagement with political and social issues, themes that would continue to inform and inspire her art throughout her career.

The influence of Diego Rivera and his communist ideals on her beliefs

Frida Kahlo's life was deeply intertwined with the political landscape of Mexico, a country grappling with revolution, social upheaval, and a burgeoning sense of national identity. While her artistic genius blossomed independently, her encounter with Diego Rivera, a renowned muralist and staunch communist, significantly shaped her political worldview and infused her art with a powerful social commentary.

Rivera, a prominent figure in the Mexican Communist Party, brought with him a fervent belief in social justice, class struggle, and the need for a radical transformation of society. His murals, often adorned with images of workers, peasants, and revolutionary figures, served as a powerful visual platform for his communist ideology. He saw art as a tool to educate and inspire the masses, challenging the status quo and advocating for a more equitable society.

Frida, a young and impressionable artist, was captivated by Rivera's passion and commitment to his beliefs. Their relationship, both personal and artistic, was a crucible of intellectual exchange and political debate. She was drawn to his radical ideas, his unwavering support for the working class, and his vision of a more just world. This influence found its way into her own artwork, albeit in a more personal and introspective manner.

While Frida's political convictions evolved throughout her life, she was initially drawn to the communist cause. She saw in it a reflection of her own struggles against social injustice, patriarchal structures, and the oppression of the working class. She embraced the idea of a classless society, where power and resources would be equitably distributed, and where individuals would be free from the constraints of capitalist exploitation.

This early engagement with communist ideals found expression in her paintings, often imbued with a sense of social realism. She portrayed the plight of the working class, the struggles of women, and the injustices of the capitalist system. Her self-portraits, while deeply personal, often served as metaphors for broader social issues, her body becoming a vessel for both individual and collective suffering.

For instance, the painting "*Self-Portrait with Thorn Necklace and Hummingbird*" (1940) can be interpreted as an allegorical representation of Frida's own struggles as a woman in a patriarchal society, her body adorned with symbols of pain and sacrifice. The hummingbird, a symbol of freedom and resilience, signifies her ability to rise above adversity. The thorn necklace, however, represents the oppressive weight of social expectations and the burden of her own personal struggles.

The communist influence on Frida's art went beyond mere thematic exploration. Rivera's emphasis on the use of art as a vehicle for social change resonated deeply with her. She saw art as a powerful weapon in the fight for justice, capable of challenging the dominant narrative and awakening the consciousness of the masses. Her art, while deeply personal and introspective, became a potent tool for social commentary, challenging established norms and advocating for a more equitable world.

It's important to note that Frida's political views were complex and ever-evolving. While she embraced communist ideals during her early years, her later life saw her distance herself from strict political affiliations. However, the influence of Rivera and his communist ideals remained a significant factor in her artistic and political development, shaping her worldview and infusing her work with a potent social conscience.

Her early artistic experimentation and exploration of different styles

While Frida Kahlo's artistic genius is undeniably linked to her later surrealist masterpieces, her early creative journey was a vibrant tapestry of experimentation and exploration. This period, marked by a passionate thirst for artistic expression and a relentless search for her own voice, saw her dabble in diverse styles, from the traditional to the avant-garde, laying the groundwork for the unique and powerful style that would later define her.

Frida's artistic awakening coincided with the turbulent political climate of Mexico during the 1920s, a period marked by the Mexican Revolution. This tumultuous era profoundly influenced her worldview and artistic sensibilities, instilling in her a deep sense of nationalism and a commitment to depicting the struggles and aspirations of the working class. In her early works, this social consciousness manifested through her portrayal of the lives of everyday Mexicans, with an emphasis on rural scenes, indigenous culture, and the realities of poverty and hardship.

Her early artistic influences were diverse and eclectic, reflecting her multifaceted personality and intellectual curiosity. Her father, Guillermo Kahlo, a photographer and ardent admirer of the photographic realism of the 19th century, instilled in her a meticulous approach to detail and a keen eye for capturing the essence of reality. Her mother, Matilde Calderón, a devoutly religious woman, introduced her to the world of religious iconography, which would later find its way into her paintings through her use of symbolic imagery and her exploration of themes of life, death, and spirituality.

However, Frida's artistic path was not solely shaped by traditional influences. She was also deeply inspired by the contemporary art scene in Mexico, particularly the burgeoning Mexican Muralist movement. The vibrant murals of Diego Rivera, José Clemente Orozco, and David Alfaro Siqueiros, depicting scenes of the Mexican Revolution and celebrating the country's cultural heritage, captivated Frida's imagination and sparked a desire to contribute to the artistic landscape of her homeland. Their emphasis on large-scale narratives and bold, expressive imagery resonated with Frida's desire to create art that was both socially conscious and visually powerful.

Frida's early artistic experimentation was marked by a desire to break free from the constraints of traditional art forms. She experimented with various mediums, from oils and watercolors to gouache and tempera, exploring different textures, techniques, and color palettes. She was drawn to the vibrant colors and bold lines of Mexican folk art, incorporating elements of indigenous symbolism and traditional motifs into her paintings. This fusion of traditional and modern elements reflected her own unique perspective on Mexican identity, blending her heritage with her contemporary artistic sensibilities.

Frida's early works also saw her explore the power of realism in capturing the human experience. She meticulously rendered portraits of ordinary Mexicans, capturing their expressions, their struggles, and their resilience in the face of adversity. These paintings reflected her deep empathy for the working class and her desire to give voice to the marginalized and forgotten.

While Frida's early paintings showcased a commitment to realism and social commentary, they also hinted at the surrealist tendencies that would later define her artistic style. Her portraits, particularly her self-portraits, often featured a blend of reality and fantasy, with dreamlike imagery, symbolic objects, and a distorted sense of space and time. This early exploration of the surreal would pave the way for her later masterpieces, where reality and fantasy became inextricably intertwined, reflecting the depths of her inner world and her complex relationship with the world around her.

Frida's artistic experimentation in these early years was not just about finding her own voice; it was about forging a unique path for herself in the art world. She refused to conform to the expectations of traditional art forms or to be pigeonholed into a single style. Instead, she embraced her own creative instincts, allowing her artistic journey to be guided by her personal experiences, her political convictions, and her profound connection to Mexican culture. This unwavering commitment to self-expression and artistic freedom laid the groundwork for the revolutionary artist she would become, forever changing the landscape of art history and inspiring generations of artists and art lovers around the world.

Chapter 4: A Meeting of Minds and Hearts:

Meeting Diego Rivera and their turbulent, passionate relationship

The year was 1922, a time of immense change and upheaval in Mexico. The country was still recovering from the tumultuous Mexican Revolution, and a new era of artistic and cultural expression was dawning. It was in this vibrant atmosphere that a young, aspiring artist named Frida Kahlo crossed paths with the legendary muralist, Diego Rivera, a man who would forever alter the course of her life.

Their first encounter was a moment of intense artistic attraction. Frida, with her fiery spirit and unique vision, was immediately captivated by Diego's bold, politically charged murals, which depicted the struggles and triumphs of the Mexican people. She saw in him a kindred soul, a fellow artist who understood the power of art as a tool for social and political change.

Diego, on the other hand, was drawn to Frida's fierce intelligence, her unwavering spirit, and her unapologetic individuality. He was captivated by her bold style and the raw emotion that poured out of her artwork, recognizing a kindred spirit in her artistic rebellion.

Theirs was a love affair that burned with the intensity of a thousand suns, a passionate whirlwind of art, politics, and unyielding desire. However, their relationship was far from simple. It was marked by a turbulent undercurrent, a constant dance between fiery passion and deep-seated insecurities. Theirs was a love that tested the boundaries of both art and human relationships.

Diego's infidelity became a constant source of pain for Frida. He was a notorious philanderer, his heart often straying from their marriage despite his deep love for Frida. Frida, in turn, found solace and support in other relationships, often finding solace in the arms of other artists and intellectuals.

Despite their turbulent love affair, Diego played a pivotal role in Frida's artistic development. He introduced her to the world of Mexican muralism, inspiring her to explore the power of art as a platform for social commentary and political activism. His influence can be seen in her use of bold colors, strong imagery, and the exploration of themes of national identity and cultural heritage.

Frida's art became a testament to their complex relationship. Her self-portraits, often infused with symbolism and allegory, reflected the turmoil of their love. The presence of thorns, blood, and anatomical imagery in her work speaks volumes about the pain and anguish she endured in their passionate but tumultuous union.

Their relationship, a mix of fiery passion, deep affection, and undeniable pain, shaped both their lives and their art.

While their marriage was a complex tapestry of joy and sorrow, their love for each other, their shared artistic vision, and their unwavering support of one another created a unique legacy that continues to inspire generations of artists and lovers around the world.

The role of Diego Rivera's influence on her artistic development

Diego Rivera, a towering figure in the Mexican muralist movement, played a pivotal role in shaping Frida Kahlo's artistic trajectory, both directly and indirectly. Their tempestuous relationship, marked by intense passion and frequent conflicts, deeply impacted her artistic sensibility and aesthetic choices. While Kahlo's art undeniably sprang from her own unique vision, Rivera's presence in her life undeniably left an indelible mark on her work.

One of the most obvious ways Rivera influenced Kahlo was through the introduction to Mexican muralism, a movement deeply rooted in national identity and social commentary. Rivera's murals, grand and monumental, celebrated Mexican history, culture, and working-class struggles. Kahlo, initially drawn to the emotional intensity of his paintings, was further captivated by their scale and public engagement. Rivera's artistic philosophy, emphasizing the power of art as a means of social change and cultural expression, resonated with Kahlo's own burgeoning political and social consciousness. This exposure to his aesthetic and thematic concerns undoubtedly contributed to Kahlo's own exploration of Mexican identity, her engagement with the social and political landscape, and her use of vibrant, symbolic imagery.

Beyond the broader artistic context, Rivera's influence extended to specific aspects of Kahlo's art. His focus on realism, particularly in depicting the human form, influenced Kahlo's own approach to portraiture. She embraced his bold, unflinching depiction of the body, using it as a canvas to explore themes of pain, sexuality, and identity. Rivera's penchant for incorporating elements of Mexican folk art, including traditional textiles, costumes, and imagery, also found a place in Kahlo's work. She frequently integrated these elements into her self-portraits, adding a layer of cultural richness and symbolism that underscored her deep connection to her heritage.

However, Rivera's influence wasn't always a positive force in Kahlo's artistic development. Their tumultuous relationship, marked by infidelity and frequent breakups, became a constant source of pain and inspiration. Kahlo's art often reflected these emotional upheavals, showcasing themes of love, loss, and betrayal. Her self-portraits, particularly those painted during their turbulent period, often depict scenes of physical and emotional suffering, highlighting the psychological impact of Rivera's actions on her. The emotional turmoil of their relationship, while deeply personal, provided fertile ground for Kahlo's artistic explorations, driving her to confront themes of identity, vulnerability, and the complexities of human relationships. In a sense, Rivera's absence and infidelity, while painful, served as a catalyst for Kahlo's artistic expression, pushing her to delve deeper into her own internal landscape.

Ultimately, while Rivera's influence was undeniable, Kahlo's artistic vision remained deeply personal. Her art transcended his influence, evolving into a unique and powerful form of self-expression. Her use of symbolism, her exploration of surrealism, and her unflinching portrayal of her own physical and emotional struggles set her apart as a singular artist. However, the encounter with Rivera's world of murals, his social consciousness, and his stylistic choices undoubtedly played a role in shaping the direction of her artistic journey. While Kahlo may have forged her own path, her artistic development was deeply intertwined with the presence of Diego Rivera, both as a mentor and a source of inspiration and pain.

Their early artistic collaborations and the impact of Diego's murals

The meeting of Frida Kahlo and Diego Rivera in 1928 marked the beginning of a tempestuous and influential chapter in both their lives and artistic careers. Diego, already a renowned muralist, was an established figure in the Mexican art world, while Frida was a young and aspiring artist still finding her voice. Their artistic collaboration, however, was not a simple sharing of talents but a complex interplay of influences, admiration, and creative friction.

Diego's monumental murals, which adorned public spaces in Mexico City and other cities, were a powerful force in shaping Frida's artistic vision. His murals, imbued with a sense of nationalism, socialism, and revolutionary spirit, reflected the themes of Mexican identity, indigenous heritage, and labor struggles that would deeply resonate with Frida. These themes, which Diego expressed through his murals, would become integral elements in Frida's own art.

In the early days of their relationship, Diego's influence on Frida's artistic development was undeniable. He encouraged her to explore realism, symbolism, and the power of visual storytelling in her work. He also introduced her to the world of Mexican folklore, mythology, and indigenous traditions, which would become recurring motifs in her art.

Frida, however, was not simply a passive recipient of Diego's influence. She brought her own unique perspective and artistic sensibilities to their collaboration. Her keen eye for detail, her fascination with anatomy and the human form, and her deeply personal exploration of pain, suffering, and the female experience enriched their artistic dialogue.

One of their most notable collaborations was the creation of Frida's self-portrait "The Two Fridas." This painting, which depicts two versions of Frida, reflects their complex and intertwined relationship. One Frida, dressed in a traditional Mexican tehuana dress, represents her connection to her Mexican heritage, while the other, with a dissected heart, symbolizes her vulnerability and the emotional turmoil she experienced in their relationship. The painting also showcases Frida's developing mastery of surrealism, a style that would become her trademark.

Their early collaborations were not without challenges. Frida's intense personality and independent spirit clashed with Diego's domineering nature. Their relationship, both personal and professional, was marked by jealousy, infidelity, and intense emotional battles. These struggles, however, also fueled their creative fire, resulting in powerful and deeply personal works of art.

In conclusion, the impact of Diego Rivera's murals on Frida Kahlo's early artistic development was profound. His monumental works, which celebrated Mexican identity and revolutionary ideals, inspired Frida to explore themes of nationalism, social justice, and the female experience. However, Frida's collaboration with Diego was not simply a passive acceptance of his influence. She brought her own unique perspective and artistic sensibilities to their work, creating a rich and complex dialogue that pushed the boundaries of art and explored the depths of their turbulent relationship. Their early collaborations, a blend of admiration, creative friction, and personal struggles, paved the way for Frida's emergence as a visionary artist whose work would become a symbol of female strength, resilience, and artistic brilliance.

Part II: The Rise of a Visionary

Chapter 5: Self-Portrait as a Revolution:

Her early self-portraits and the emergence of her unique artistic voice

Frida Kahlo's self-portraits are not mere depictions of her physical appearance; they are profound explorations of her inner world, her struggles, and her triumphs. They are the foundation upon which her artistic voice, a raw and unflinchingly honest one, was built. It was through these self-portraits that she began to challenge conventional art practices, embrace the complexities of her identity, and unveil the depths of her pain and resilience.

Kahlo's early self-portraits, painted in the 1920s and early 1930s, are marked by a striking vulnerability and a sense of self-discovery. These early works were often painted during periods of intense physical and emotional suffering, a direct result of the bus accident that had left her with chronic pain and a fractured body. In these early works, she delved into the complex relationship between her physical and emotional experiences. In *Self-Portrait with Thorn Necklace and Hummingbird* (1940), she captures the anguish of pain through the thorny necklace that constricts her neck, symbolizing her constant struggle with physical and emotional torment. She explores the themes of mortality and suffering through the use of symbolic imagery, such as the thorn necklace, the hummingbird, and the anatomical details that reveal the scars of her injuries. These early self-portraits established her signature style, characterized by vivid colors, bold outlines, and the fusion of realism and symbolism.

Kahlo's self-portraits were not only explorations of physical pain but also profound explorations of her identity. In *The Two Fridas* (1939), she presents a dual portrait, showcasing the two sides of her personality. One Frida, dressed in a European-inspired outfit, represents her more conventional and idealized self, while the other, wearing a traditional Mexican dress, embodies her cultural roots and her rebellious nature. This self-portrait highlights the ongoing internal conflict she experienced between her Mexican heritage and the influence of European culture. By representing her internal struggles through this dual portrait, she challenges the notion of a singular identity and embraces the multiplicity of her being.

Kahlo's unique artistic voice resonated with the spirit of Mexican identity. She seamlessly intertwined her personal experiences with the political and social upheavals of her time, drawing inspiration from the Mexican Revolution and its embrace of indigenous culture. Her self-portraits, often depicting her in traditional Mexican attire, became powerful symbols of national pride and cultural identity. *Self-Portrait with Thorn Necklace and Hummingbird* (1940) and *Self-Portrait with Monkey* (1938) showcased the fusion of Mexican folk art traditions, vibrant colors, and symbolic imagery. She used the imagery of the hummingbird and the monkey to represent her rebellious spirit and connection to the natural world, while incorporating elements of traditional Mexican clothing and embroidery to celebrate her heritage. Through these self-portraits, Kahlo established a distinct style that blended personal expression with a deep connection to her cultural roots.

Kahlo's early self-portraits were a testament to her raw artistic talent and her unwavering commitment to self-expression. They were a powerful departure from the traditional art world, where female artists were often relegated to portraying domestic scenes or subjects considered "feminine." In contrast, Kahlo's self-portraits were boldly personal, challenging the boundaries of gender roles and societal expectations. They were a testament to her strength, her vulnerability, and her unwavering commitment to embracing her complexities. Through these self-portraits, she established a unique artistic voice that resonated with generations to come.

Exploration of identity, womanhood, and the female experience

Frida Kahlo's self-portraits are more than just artistic representations; they are profound explorations of identity, womanhood, and the female experience. Through her unflinching gaze and vivid imagery, Kahlo challenged conventional notions of beauty, femininity, and the very definition of what it meant to be a woman in a patriarchal society.

Kahlo's self-portraits became her battleground, her canvas for confronting the physical and emotional turmoil she endured. She used her art to reclaim her body, often depicted wounded, bleeding, and raw, defying societal expectations that women should be delicate and demure. The inclusion of her unibrow and mustache, features often considered masculine, challenged the very definition of beauty. These elements became symbols of her defiance, a statement of her refusal to conform to traditional standards of femininity.

In many of her self-portraits, Kahlo incorporated traditional Mexican clothing, particularly tehuana dresses. This was a conscious choice, a way to embrace her Mexican heritage and connect with the strength and resilience of indigenous women. These dresses, with their vibrant colors and intricate embroidery, became symbolic of a powerful, vibrant, and unapologetically feminine identity.

Kahlo's self-portraits often depicted her surrounded by flowers, a motif that holds multiple layers of meaning. Flowers symbolize beauty, fragility, and the cyclical nature of life and death. In Kahlo's work, they are not just decorative elements but powerful symbols of her connection to nature, her pain, and her resilience. In paintings like "The Two Fridas", the flowers, both blooming and decaying, represent the dualities within her, the pain and joy, the strength and vulnerability.

Beyond the imagery, Kahlo's self-portraits often featured powerful symbolism that explored the complexities of womanhood. For instance, her iconic self-portrait "The Broken Column" depicts her body as a broken column, physically and emotionally shattered. This image, with its stark imagery of pain and suffering, became a powerful metaphor for the physical and emotional pain that women often endure, particularly in a patriarchal society.

Through her art, Kahlo challenged traditional gender roles and the expectations placed upon women. She celebrated female strength, sexuality, and self-determination, while refusing to be defined by societal norms or by her physical limitations. Her paintings became a platform for expressing her own unique voice, a voice that resonated with countless women who saw themselves reflected in her struggles, triumphs, and enduring spirit.

Frida Kahlo's self-portraits are a testament to the power of art as a tool for self-expression, identity exploration, and a challenge to societal norms. Her works continue to inspire and empower women, reminding us of the strength and resilience that lie within each of us.

The use of vivid imagery, symbolism, and surrealism

Frida Kahlo's artistic language was a potent blend of realism, symbolism, and surrealism, reflecting her unique perspective on life, pain, and identity. Her paintings are a tapestry of vivid imagery, evocative symbolism, and dreamlike surrealism, weaving together personal narratives with universal themes of suffering, resilience, and the complexities of the human experience.

Vivid Imagery: Frida Kahlo's paintings are filled with intensely vibrant and often jarring imagery, drawing the viewer into the raw and intimate world of her experiences. She wielded color with a boldness that mirrored her spirit, employing stark contrasts and saturated hues to convey her emotions and the intensity of her physical and emotional landscapes. From the brilliant red of blood and the deep blues of the night sky to the warm ochre of her skin and the lush greens of Mexican flora, her palette mirrored the complexities of her inner world.

Symbolic Language: Kahlo's paintings are rich with symbolism, each element carefully chosen to convey deeper meanings. Her iconic unibrow, for instance, represented her defiance of conventional beauty standards and her embrace of her individuality. Her use of thorns, often entwined with flowers, symbolized the duality of pain and beauty, reflecting the constant interplay of suffering and resilience in her life. The presence of anatomical imagery - hearts, spines, and broken bones - underscored the physical pain she endured and the ways it permeated her artistic expression.

Surrealist Exploration: While Frida Kahlo wasn't a strict adherent to the surrealist movement, she embraced its principles of exploring dreams, subconscious desires, and the blurring of reality and fantasy. Her self-portraits often depict her in fantastical settings, surrounded by dreamlike elements that allude to her inner world. The image of a butterfly emerging from her body in "The Two Fridas" (1939) embodies this surrealist aesthetic, symbolizing the duality of her identity and her yearning for healing and transformation.

The Power of Self-Portraiture: Frida Kahlo's self-portraits are perhaps her most powerful works, serving as both windows into her soul and artistic statements. She utilized the self-portrait as a means of exploring her identity, her physical and emotional struggles, and her complex relationship with her body and the world. In these self-portraits, her intense gaze, often accompanied by a melancholic expression, speaks to her inner turmoil, while the use of symbolism and surrealism amplifies the emotional depth and personal meaning she invested in each work.

Beyond the Personal: While deeply personal, Frida Kahlo's use of vivid imagery, symbolism, and surrealism resonated with a universal human experience. Her art transcended the confines of personal narrative to become a powerful exploration of themes of identity, pain, resilience, and the complexities of the human condition. She explored these themes through the lens of her Mexican heritage, infusing her work with the rich colors, symbols, and traditions of her culture.

Through her unique and powerful visual language, Frida Kahlo transformed her personal struggles into universal art. Her paintings continue to inspire and move viewers, inviting them to confront the complexities of life, death, and the human experience with honesty, courage, and a profound appreciation for the beauty that can emerge from suffering.

Chapter 6: Pain and Beauty: The Symbolism of Suffering:

Pain as a recurring theme in her work, reflecting her physical and emotional struggles

Frida Kahlo's art was a profound reflection of her tumultuous life, a canvas where she poured her pain, struggles, and triumphs. While her vibrant colors and surreal imagery often captivated viewers, a closer examination reveals a recurring theme that permeated her work: **pain**. This was not merely a stylistic element but a visceral expression of the physical and emotional suffering that defined her existence.

Frida's life was marked by a series of debilitating accidents and chronic illnesses. At the young age of 18, she was involved in a devastating bus crash that left her with severe injuries, including a broken spinal column, a fractured pelvis, and a crushed foot. This event became a pivotal moment in her life, forever shaping her physical and emotional landscape. The accident also triggered a cascade of health issues, including recurring bouts of pain, recurrent infections, and chronic illnesses that plagued her for the rest of her life.

Frida's art became a form of catharsis, a means of processing and expressing the profound pain she endured. Her self-portraits often depicted the physical consequences of her accident, showcasing her fractured body, her reliance on crutches, and the medical apparatuses that became her constant companions. Her iconic self-portrait titled "The Broken Column" is a poignant testament to her physical suffering. It depicts Frida as a fractured column, symbolizing her shattered body, while a nail pierces her flesh, representing the agonizing pain she experienced.

Frida's pain wasn't limited to the physical realm; it extended to the emotional sphere. Her relationship with Diego Rivera, a renowned muralist and her husband, was tempestuous and marked by infidelity and emotional turmoil. Frida's paintings often reflected the emotional wounds of her tumultuous marriage, showcasing themes of betrayal, abandonment, and heartbreak. In her self-portrait titled "The Two Fridas," she portrays two distinct versions of herself, symbolizing the duality of her emotions and the struggle to reconcile her pain with her resilience.

The use of anatomical imagery in her art became a powerful tool for expressing her internal struggles. She often depicted blood, wounds, and bodily fluids, transforming these symbols of vulnerability and suffering into elements of artistic expression. Her paintings became a visual language of pain, a raw and honest exploration of the emotional and physical turmoil she faced.

While Frida's art was deeply rooted in her own struggles, it also resonated with a broader human experience. Her unflinching portrayal of pain, her exploration of themes of suffering and mortality, and her raw emotional honesty connected with audiences on a universal level. Her art became a testament to the resilience of the human spirit, a reminder that even amidst profound pain, there is beauty, strength, and a desire to live.

Frida's ability to transform her pain into art was a remarkable feat. Her paintings transcended the limitations of her physical body, becoming a vessel for her emotions, her thoughts, and her innermost struggles. They became a powerful reminder that pain is a universal human experience, and that art can serve as a profound tool for processing, expressing, and ultimately transcending it.

The use of anatomical imagery, blood, and bodily fluids

Within the intricate tapestry of Frida Kahlo's artistic universe, the visceral imagery of **anatomical details**, **blood**, and **bodily fluids** emerges as a stark and unflinching reflection of her personal struggles and artistic vision. This deliberate use of unflinching realism, often bordering on the grotesque, is a testament to Kahlo's unapologetic approach to portraying the raw, unfiltered experience of pain and suffering.

Her iconic **self-portraits** frequently feature graphic depictions of her physical injuries, particularly those sustained in the devastating bus accident that marked a turning point in her life. In works like *"The Broken Column"* (1944), Kahlo depicts herself as a broken figure, with a visible spine bisected by a **column** that represents her pain and fragility. The **blood** that flows from the column symbolizes the constant suffering that she endured.

The **anatomical imagery** is not merely a literal representation of physical pain; it serves as a metaphorical exploration of the emotional and psychological wounds that plagued her. The **blood**, often depicted in vivid hues of crimson and scarlet, becomes a symbol of both physical and emotional anguish. It is a testament to the deep connection between the body and the mind, and the way in which physical pain can resonate on a profound emotional level.

Kahlo's use of **bodily fluids** is equally evocative and unapologetic. In works like *"Henry Ford Hospital"* (1932), she portrays herself surrounded by **blood**, **tears**, and **medical instruments**, creating a visceral scene that reflects her experiences with miscarriage and the medical interventions that she underwent. These depictions are not meant to be graphic or shocking for their own sake; instead, they are a powerful testament to Kahlo's unwavering desire to confront the reality of her suffering and to explore its profound impact on her identity.

Beyond their literal interpretations, the **anatomical imagery**, **blood**, and **bodily fluids** in Kahlo's art transcend the physical realm to delve into the depths of human emotion and experience. They represent the fragility of the human body, the constant struggle for resilience, and the profound connection between the physical and the emotional.

Her use of these stark and powerful elements is a testament to Kahlo's artistic courage and her relentless pursuit of truth and authenticity. They are a reminder that pain is an integral part of life, and that by confronting it head-on, we can find strength, resilience, and ultimately, a deeper understanding of ourselves.

Exploring themes of life, death, and the fragility of the human body

Frida Kahlo's life was inextricably linked to pain and suffering. From the devastating bus accident that fractured her body and left her with chronic pain to the numerous surgeries and illnesses she endured throughout her life, her physical fragility became a central theme in her art. This chapter delves into how Kahlo's work not only reflects her own personal struggles with mortality but also explores universal themes of life, death, and the fragility of the human body.

Kahlo's art often depicts anatomical imagery, revealing her deep fascination with the human form and its vulnerability. She frequently portrays blood, bodily fluids, and exposed organs, using these graphic elements to confront viewers with the harsh realities of the body's fragility. In her self-portrait, *The Broken Column* (1944), she presents herself as a shattered statue, her spine fractured and held together by a metal column, symbolizing the constant pain that permeated her existence. This stark image underscores the precariousness of the human form and its susceptibility to injury and decay.

Beyond the physical, Kahlo's exploration of the body's fragility extends to its emotional and psychological vulnerability. Her paintings often express her internal struggles with pain, loss, and mortality. In *Henry Ford Hospital* (1932), she depicts her hospitalization after a miscarriage, surrounded by medical instruments and symbols of her suffering. This haunting self-portrait reveals the deep emotional pain she endured, emphasizing the vulnerability of the human spirit in the face of loss and heartbreak.

Kahlo's art not only confronts the harsh realities of pain and suffering but also celebrates the resilience of the human spirit. Her works often depict vibrant imagery, symbols of life, and elements of Mexican folklore, suggesting a deep connection to the cyclical nature of life and death. In *The Two Fridas* (1939), she portrays two versions of herself, one with a bleeding heart connected to the other by shared veins, symbolizing the interconnectedness of life and death. This dual representation reflects Kahlo's own internal struggle with her mortality while also suggesting a sense of acceptance and transcendence.

Kahlo's exploration of life, death, and the fragility of the human body is not merely a personal reflection of her own experiences. She uses these themes to connect with universal human experiences, engaging viewers with questions about mortality, resilience, and the meaning of existence. Her art serves as a powerful testament to the strength and vulnerability of the human condition, reminding us of our own shared fragility while celebrating the enduring spirit of life.

Chapter 7: The Surrealist Embrace:

Her connection with surrealism and its influence on her artistic practice

Frida Kahlo's connection with surrealism is a complex and fascinating one. While she never formally aligned herself with the surrealist movement, her art deeply resonated with the movement's core principles, particularly its exploration of the subconscious, dreams, and the merging of reality and fantasy. This chapter delves into the intricate relationship between Kahlo and surrealism, examining the ways in which the movement influenced her artistic practice and how her unique vision contributed to the broader surrealist discourse.

While Kahlo's art often contained elements of the surreal, she wasn't simply imitating the style of surrealist artists. Instead, she drew upon the movement's principles to create a unique and personal visual language that reflected her own experiences and emotions. Kahlo's art was not simply about the fantastic and bizarre, but rather about using those elements to express the deep-seated realities of her own pain, suffering, and resilience.

One of the key ways in which surrealism influenced Kahlo's art was through its emphasis on the subconscious. Surrealists believed that the subconscious mind held a vast reservoir of imagery and ideas that could be accessed through dreams, free association, and other techniques. Kahlo, deeply affected by the bus accident that left her with chronic pain and a fractured body, often drew inspiration from her own dreams and hallucinations. Her self-portraits often depicted her body distorted and fragmented, reflecting the disorientation and physical trauma she endured. For example, in The Two Fridas (1939), Kahlo depicts herself as two separate figures, one with a bleeding heart, revealing the deep emotional turmoil and division she experienced.

Another key aspect of surrealism that influenced Kahlo's work was its exploration of the relationship between reality and fantasy. Surrealists sought to break down the boundaries between the rational and the irrational, the conscious and the unconscious. They often used jarring juxtapositions of objects and imagery to create a sense of dreamlike disorientation. Kahlo embraced this approach, merging elements of reality with her own personal mythology. She often incorporated symbolic objects and imagery into her paintings, imbuing them with personal meaning. For instance, in The Broken Column (1944), a steel spine replaces her own spine, representing the weight of her physical pain and the psychological burden she carried.

While Kahlo's connection to surrealism was not a simple adoption of the movement's principles, it was a complex and dynamic interplay between her own personal experiences and the broader artistic landscape. She embraced the movement's fascination with the subconscious, its desire to disrupt the boundaries between reality and fantasy, and its focus on expressing personal truths through symbolic imagery. However, Kahlo's surrealism was distinctly her own, infused with a fierce independence, a profound sense of self-awareness, and a unique vision that challenged both traditional artistic conventions and societal norms.

In conclusion, Frida Kahlo's relationship with surrealism was not one of simple adherence, but rather a dynamic exchange between her personal experiences and the movement's core principles. Her art, while imbued with surrealist elements, was ultimately an expression of her own deeply personal struggles, her enduring spirit, and her desire to express the complexities of the female experience. It was through this unique lens that Kahlo's art resonated with surrealism, yet transcended its boundaries, forging a path uniquely her own.

The merging of reality and fantasy in her self-portraits

Frida Kahlo's self-portraits are not mere reflections of her physical appearance; they are portals into the intricate landscape of her mind, where the lines between reality and fantasy blur and intertwine. This unique artistic approach, often attributed to her affinity for Surrealism, allowed Kahlo to express the complexities of her inner world, her physical and emotional struggles, and her unwavering spirit in the face of adversity.

In her self-portraits, Kahlo seamlessly blends elements of her lived experience with surreal imagery, creating a visual tapestry that defies conventional artistic norms. She often depicts herself in symbolic settings, surrounded by objects that hold personal significance, and infused with dreamlike elements that speak to her subconscious desires and anxieties. The resulting artwork transcends the boundaries of mere portraiture, becoming an intimate exploration of her inner world, her identity, and her relentless struggle for self-definition.

One striking example is her iconic self-portrait, *The Two Fridas* (1939). This powerful work depicts two Fridas, both connected by a shared artery that is severed by a single surgical clamp. The Frida on the left, dressed in European clothing, represents the idealized, more conventional version of herself, while the Frida on the right, adorned with traditional Mexican attire, embodies her deeper connection to her roots and her rebellious spirit. The severed artery symbolizes the pain of her separation from Diego Rivera and the emotional turmoil she experienced during that time.

Another compelling example of this merging of reality and fantasy is her self-portrait, *The Broken Column* (1944). In this painting, Kahlo depicts herself as a human column, her spine fractured, with nails protruding from her body, symbolizing the physical pain and suffering she endured throughout her life. This self-portrait, painted during a period of intense physical and emotional distress, serves as a poignant reminder of her resilience and her ability to transform pain into art.

Kahlo's self-portraits often feature symbolic objects that hold personal meaning. Flowers, a recurring motif in her work, represent life, growth, and beauty, but also fragility and mortality. The thorns on roses, for example, symbolize the pain and suffering that often accompany love and life's complexities. In *Self-Portrait with Thorn Necklace and Hummingbird* (1940), Kahlo uses a necklace of thorns and a hummingbird to symbolize the duality of love and pain, reminding viewers of the complexities of human emotions and the interconnectedness of joy and sorrow.

Furthermore, Kahlo's self-portraits are often infused with a sense of dreamlike reality, blurring the lines between the conscious and the subconscious. In *The Dream* (1940), she depicts herself asleep in a bed, surrounded by symbolic objects that represent her anxieties and desires. The painting's surreal atmosphere transports the viewer into the realm of her dreams, allowing them to glimpse the complexities of her inner world.

By merging reality and fantasy in her self-portraits, Frida Kahlo created a unique artistic language that allowed her to confront her personal struggles, celebrate her Mexican heritage, and explore the depths of her own identity. Her paintings serve as a testament to her unwavering spirit, her ability to transform pain into art, and her enduring legacy as a feminist icon and one of the most significant artists of the 20th century.

The exploration of dreams, subconscious desires, and personal mythology

Frida Kahlo's art, while deeply rooted in her personal experiences and physical struggles, also ventured into the realm of dreams, subconscious desires, and personal mythology. This exploration, heavily influenced by surrealism, allowed her to transcend the boundaries of reality and delve into the depths of her inner world.

In her self-portraits, Kahlo often depicted herself surrounded by fantastical imagery, merging reality with the surreal. This fusion of the tangible and the intangible reflects her desire to express her inner landscape, revealing the complexities of her subconscious. Her dreams, often filled with pain, longing, and the weight of her physical limitations, became a central motif in her work.

For instance, in the painting *The Two Fridas*, two versions of Kahlo stand side by side, connected by a single artery, symbolic of their shared experiences and internal conflict. One Frida, adorned with traditional Mexican clothing, represents her connection to her heritage and roots. The other Frida, adorned with a medical corset, symbolizes her physical pain and the limitations imposed by her body. This juxtaposition of contrasting identities reflects the internal struggles and contradictions that Kahlo grappled with throughout her life.

Beyond dreams, Kahlo's art explored the realm of subconscious desires, often expressed through powerful and evocative symbols. The recurring motif of thorns and blood in her work embodies both the pain she endured and the strength she found within herself. These symbols, imbued with both physical and emotional significance, serve as powerful metaphors for her struggles and triumphs.

In her painting *The Broken Column*, Kahlo depicts herself with a broken column replacing her spine, symbolizing the profound impact of her bus accident on her physical and emotional well-being. The column, a symbol of strength and support, is shattered, representing the fragility of her body and the enduring pain she carried within. This painting is not simply a depiction of physical injury but a powerful metaphor for the internal struggles she faced and the burden of pain she carried.

Furthermore, Kahlo's art embraced personal mythology, weaving narratives that transcended the literal and delved into the realm of the symbolic. This approach allowed her to create a unique visual language, reflecting her personal experiences and offering insights into her beliefs and worldview.

In *The Dream*, Kahlo paints a scene where she is lying in a bed surrounded by surreal elements, including a fetus, a heart, and a pelvic bone. This dream-like setting reflects her fears of motherhood, the pain of her physical limitations, and the constant presence of mortality. The juxtaposition of these elements creates a powerful and unsettling image, reflecting the anxieties and subconscious desires that plagued her.

Through her exploration of dreams, subconscious desires, and personal mythology, Frida Kahlo crafted a powerful and evocative body of work. Her paintings, filled with surreal imagery, symbolic elements, and personal narratives, provide a glimpse into the depths of her inner world, revealing the complexities of her life, her struggles, and her unwavering spirit.

Chapter 8: Mexico in Her Art:

Deep connection to Mexican culture, identity, and indigenous heritage

Frida Kahlo's art was profoundly rooted in her Mexican identity. Born in Coyoacán, a historic neighborhood in Mexico City, Kahlo was steeped in the vibrant tapestry of Mexican culture, a blend of indigenous traditions, colonial influences, and revolutionary spirit. This deep connection to her heritage permeated her art, transforming her canvases into powerful expressions of Mexican pride, cultural identity, and folklore.

From a young age, Kahlo was exposed to the rich visual language of Mexican folk art, with its vivid colors, intricate patterns, and symbolic imagery. Her father, a photographer, instilled in her an appreciation for capturing the essence of life, while her mother, a devout Catholic, introduced her to the world of religious iconography and traditional beliefs. This upbringing fostered a deep understanding of the symbolic nature of art and its power to convey complex emotions and ideas.

The Mexican Revolution, which erupted in 1910, left a lasting impact on Kahlo's worldview. She witnessed the struggle for national liberation firsthand, becoming acutely aware of the social and political injustices plaguing her country. This experience instilled in her a sense of social consciousness and a passion for advocating for the marginalized and oppressed.

Kahlo's connection to Mexico's indigenous heritage was particularly profound. She felt a strong affinity with the ancient Aztec civilization, its mythology, and its artistic traditions. This fascination is evident in her paintings, where she frequently incorporates pre-Columbian motifs, such as the Teotihuacan pyramids, Mayan deities, and Aztec symbols.

The tehuana dress, a traditional garment worn by women from the Isthmus of Tehuantepec, became an integral part of Kahlo's personal style and a recurring element in her self-portraits. This dress, with its vibrant colors, intricate embroidery, and flowing silhouette, symbolized the strength, independence, and beauty of Mexican women.

Beyond the visual elements, Kahlo's art also explored themes deeply connected to Mexico's cultural identity. Her paintings often depicted scenes from everyday life in Mexico, capturing the vibrancy, the struggles, and the spirit of the people. She celebrated the resilience of the Mexican spirit, the beauty of the landscape, and the richness of the country's folklore.

One of the most prominent examples of Kahlo's Mexican identity in her art is the painting "The Two Fridas" (1939). This iconic work depicts two versions of Kahlo, one with a European heart and the other with a Mexican heart, representing the duality of her identity. The European Frida, connected to her European father, is seen as frail and vulnerable, while the Mexican Frida, connected to her indigenous heritage, is depicted as strong and resilient. This painting underscores the complex interplay of cultural influences in Kahlo's life and art.

Frida Kahlo's art was a powerful testament to her profound connection to Mexico. Her paintings celebrated Mexican culture, explored its complexities, and gave voice to the struggles and triumphs of the Mexican people. By blending traditional Mexican motifs with personal experiences and revolutionary ideals, Kahlo created a unique artistic language that resonated with audiences worldwide, making her a cultural icon and a symbol of Mexican pride.

Representation of traditional Mexican clothing, textiles, and flora

Frida Kahlo's artistic canvas was a vibrant tapestry interwoven with the threads of her Mexican heritage. This was evident in her prolific use of traditional Mexican clothing, textiles, and flora, which became potent symbols in her self-portraits and broader artistic expressions. By incorporating these elements, Kahlo paid homage to her roots, showcasing the rich cultural tapestry of her homeland and asserting a strong sense of national pride within her work.

The *tehuana* **dress**, a traditional garment from the Isthmus of Tehuantepec, became a recurring motif in Kahlo's self-portraits. This vibrant, intricately embroidered dress, with its flowing skirts and colorful embellishments, represented a powerful symbol of Mexican womanhood, signifying strength, independence, and cultural heritage. Kahlo's embrace of this garment, especially in self-portraits, challenged the prevailing Western notions of femininity and asserted her Mexican identity. She often adorned herself in these dresses with a strong, assertive stance, radiating a powerful femininity that stood in contrast to the passive, demure images often associated with women in Western art.

Beyond clothing, Kahlo's canvases were frequently adorned with *huipiles*, traditional handwoven blouses worn by indigenous Mexican women. These garments, often adorned with intricate embroidery and vibrant colors, served as visual reminders of Mexico's indigenous heritage. By incorporating these garments into her artwork, Kahlo celebrated the artistry and cultural significance of Mexico's indigenous communities, weaving a tapestry of cultural pride into her self-portraits and highlighting the enduring traditions of her homeland.

Another vital component of Kahlo's artistic lexicon was the use of flora, specifically the vibrant flowers and plants native to Mexico. These botanical elements, including the *cempasúchil* (marigold), the *maguey* (agave), and the *nopal* (prickly pear cactus), were more than mere decorative elements. They held deep cultural significance, often associated with *Día de los Muertos* (Day of the Dead), a Mexican holiday celebrating the lives of the deceased. This connection further emphasized Kahlo's fascination with mortality, life cycles, and the enduring spirit of the Mexican culture.

The *cempasúchil*, with its vibrant orange petals, represents the cycle of life and death, symbolizing the connection between the living and the deceased. The *maguey*, a plant used to produce tequila and pulque, holds symbolic importance in Mexican culture, representing resilience, perseverance, and the ability to thrive in harsh environments. And the *nopal*, with its prickly exterior and nourishing fruit, represents the strength and resilience of the Mexican people, their ability to adapt and flourish despite hardship.

Through her masterful use of these traditional elements, Kahlo seamlessly intertwined her personal struggles, her identity, and her deep love for her homeland. The vibrant hues, textures, and symbols derived from Mexico's rich cultural tapestry served as a visual language, creating a powerful narrative that resonated with viewers on a deeply personal and emotional level. By incorporating these elements, Kahlo challenged Western notions of art and beauty, forging a uniquely Mexican visual language that celebrated the resilience, spirit, and vibrant culture of her homeland.

Exploration of themes of national pride, cultural identity, and folklore

Frida Kahlo's artistic expression was deeply intertwined with her profound connection to Mexican culture, identity, and indigenous heritage. Her paintings were not merely canvases for artistic experimentation but powerful platforms for showcasing the richness and complexities of her national identity. Throughout her career, Kahlo consistently infused her work with elements that celebrated Mexican tradition, history, and folklore, transforming her canvases into vibrant tapestries of national pride and cultural authenticity.

One of the most prominent ways Kahlo celebrated her Mexican heritage was through her meticulous depiction of traditional Mexican clothing, textiles, and flora. The vibrant colors, intricate patterns, and symbolic significance of these elements were integral to her artistic vocabulary. In her self-portraits, she frequently adorned herself with tehuana dresses, known for their flowing fabric, intricate embroidery, and historical connection to the Isthmus of Tehuantepec in southern Mexico. These dresses were not simply fashion choices but powerful statements of her Mexican heritage, symbolizing strength, independence, and cultural pride.

The huipil, a traditional woven blouse worn by indigenous women in Mexico, also made frequent appearances in her paintings. Often seen as a symbol of femininity and cultural identity, the huipil served as a visual reminder of Kahlo's connection to her roots and her appreciation for the rich tapestry of Mexican indigenous traditions.

Kahlo's engagement with Mexican flora, particularly flowers, went beyond mere aesthetic appeal. She used flowers as powerful symbols of life, beauty, and mortality, reflecting the delicate balance between joy and sorrow, celebration and loss that permeated her life and art.

Her "Self-Portrait with Thorn Necklace and Hummingbird" (1940) stands as a prime example of her masterful fusion of symbolism and cultural reference. In this iconic portrait, Kahlo depicted herself with a delicate hummingbird, a symbol of beauty, fragility, and the fleeting nature of life, juxtaposed against the sharp thorns of a necklace that represent pain and suffering.

Beyond clothing and flora, Kahlo also delved into the heart of Mexican folklore, drawing inspiration from myths, legends, and indigenous beliefs. She incorporated elements like pre-Columbian Aztec imagery, Day of the Dead symbolism, and references to ancient rituals and deities into her art. This engagement with indigenous traditions served as a powerful testament to the enduring presence of Mexico's rich cultural heritage.

Kahlo's "The Broken Column" (1944) offers a striking example of her exploration of Mexican folklore. This powerful self-portrait depicts her with a column cracking through her body, a reference to the Aztec god Tlaloc, the god of rain and earthquakes, who was often depicted with a broken column. This symbolic merging of ancient mythology with her personal experience of pain and suffering demonstrates Kahlo's profound connection to her cultural roots and her ability to translate these traditions into her own artistic language.

In her embrace of Mexican tradition and folklore, Kahlo transcended the realm of mere artistic representation. She actively used these elements to explore themes of national pride, cultural identity, and the enduring spirit of the Mexican people. Her paintings were not simply depictions of her personal experiences, but powerful affirmations of her Mexican identity and her unwavering commitment to her cultural heritage. Through her art, she championed the beauty and complexity of Mexican culture, showcasing it to the world with both passion and respect. Her enduring legacy lies not only in her artistic brilliance but also in her ability to use her art as a platform for celebrating the vibrant tapestry of Mexican identity and its enduring cultural richness.

Part III: Love, Loss, and Resilience

Chapter 9: A Stormy Marriage:

The complexities and struggles of her relationship with Diego Rivera

The relationship between Frida Kahlo and Diego Rivera, two giants of Mexican art, was a whirlwind of passion, artistic collaboration, and ultimately, enduring heartache. It was a marriage fraught with infidelity, jealousy, and a profound mutual admiration that often teetered on the edge of destruction.

Their connection was forged in the fiery crucible of Mexico's artistic and political landscape. In 1929, Frida, a young aspiring artist, met Diego Rivera, already a celebrated muralist and a leading figure in the Mexican communist movement. Their shared passion for Mexican culture, art, and politics ignited an instant attraction that quickly blossomed into a romantic entanglement. Their union was a bold statement, a celebration of Mexican identity at a time of political and social upheaval.

Despite their shared artistic genius and political convictions, their personalities were clashing. Diego, a larger-than-life figure known for his charisma and extramarital affairs, was a stark contrast to Frida, a woman of fierce independence and unwavering self-expression. Their passion was intense, but so was their turbulence.

Diego's infidelity was a constant source of anguish for Frida. His affairs were not mere indiscretions; they were often public displays of affection and defiance that deeply wounded Frida's pride and self-esteem. She responded to his betrayals with a mixture of rage, despair, and a deep-seated need for control.

Frida's suffering, both physical and emotional, became the fuel for her art. Her self-portraits, often imbued with surreal imagery, captured the raw pain and vulnerability of their relationship. She painted torment with a boldness and honesty that startled the art world, showcasing the complexities of love, loss, and suffering.

Despite the turmoil of their relationship, Frida and Diego were deeply bound to one another. Their artistic connection remained strong, with each influencing the other's work in profound ways. Frida often drew inspiration from Diego's monumental murals, while Diego admired Frida's bold expression and unique style. They were a creative force to be reckoned with, their individual talents intertwined in a complex and often volatile dance.

Their marriage, a testament to their passion and artistic brilliance, lasted for over a decade. Throughout their tumultuous journey, they challenged societal norms and pushed the boundaries of artistic expression. Despite the pain and struggles they endured, their love for each other, their artistic connection, and their shared commitment to Mexican identity remained a constant, weaving a narrative of love, loss, and artistic brilliance that continues to resonate today.

Their love, passion, and infidelity

The tempestuous relationship between Frida Kahlo and Diego Rivera was a whirlwind of passionate love, artistic collaboration, and undeniable infidelity. Their connection was an undeniable force, a union of two powerful and complex individuals who both fiercely embraced life and art in all its messy glory.

Their initial encounter in 1927, at a party hosted by the renowned Mexican muralist, ignited an immediate spark. Diego, already a prominent figure in the art world, was immediately captivated by Frida's vibrant personality and striking beauty. Frida, at only 20, found herself drawn to Diego's charisma, artistic talent, and the power he exuded. Theirs was a relationship built on an intoxicating blend of physical attraction and intellectual stimulation, a meeting of minds and souls fueled by shared artistic vision and radical political ideologies.

Their love was intense and passionate, a force that consumed their lives, fueling both their creative endeavors and their personal struggles. They were soulmates who challenged and inspired each other, their love serving as the foundation for their collaborative art, where their artistic styles intertwined and clashed in a fascinating dance. Diego's murals, with their depictions of Mexican history and revolutionary spirit, deeply influenced Frida's own artistic exploration, pushing her to confront the themes of identity, gender, and societal expectations through her own unique lens.

But their relationship was not without its cracks. Despite their shared passion for art and revolution, Frida's independence and strength clashed with Diego's patriarchal views. Diego's infidelities, often blatant and hurtful, became a constant source of pain and heartbreak for Frida. He was a notorious philanderer, his artistic fame and charisma a magnet for women, and his emotional affairs, a constant reminder of Frida's vulnerability within the relationship.

The complexities of their relationship were reflected in Frida's art. Her self-portraits, often filled with raw emotion and symbolic imagery, served as an outlet for her anguish and anger. She painted herself with thorns intertwined with her hair, a symbol of the pain inflicted by Diego's infidelity, and her piercing gaze reflected a woman wrestling with betrayal and heartache.

Despite the constant heartache, Frida was not one to crumble under the weight of Diego's betrayals. She held her own, her spirit unyielding. Her art became a weapon, a testament to her resilience and the strength of her own convictions. She refused to be a passive victim, using her art to reclaim her agency and challenge societal expectations.

Theirs was a complex and enduring love story, a testament to the undeniable power of attraction and shared passion, despite the darkness of infidelity and the turmoil of their personal struggles. Diego and Frida, in their love and conflict, provided a powerful reflection on the complexities of human relationships and the intricate dance between love and pain. Their story remains a potent reminder of the passionate complexities that can exist within a single relationship, a love story etched in history, art, and the unwavering strength of the human spirit.

The role of Frida's strength and independence in navigating the complexities of their union

Frida Kahlo's marriage to Diego Rivera was a tempestuous affair, marked by intense passion, creative collaboration, and enduring conflicts. While Diego's fame and influence loomed large, Frida's own strength and independence were crucial in navigating the complexities of their union. This chapter delves into the ways Frida's unwavering spirit, artistic voice, and refusal to be defined by her role as Diego's wife shaped their relationship and ultimately allowed her to forge her own path as an artist and individual.

Frida, with her fierce spirit and unwavering determination, refused to be overshadowed by Diego's larger-than-life presence. She brought a powerful individuality to their partnership, refusing to simply be the woman behind the celebrated muralist. While Diego's influence on Frida's artistic journey is undeniable, it's equally important to recognize her own inherent strength and her refusal to conform to traditional expectations of a wife or muse. Frida was an artist in her own right, with a unique vision and a compelling artistic voice that demanded to be heard.

This defiance of conventional roles is evident in Frida's self-portraits, which became her signature artistic expression. They were not simply portraits of a woman but powerful statements about identity, womanhood, and the complexities of the human experience. These self-portraits, filled with vibrant colors, symbolic imagery, and unflinching honesty, were a testament to Frida's unwavering spirit and her refusal to be defined by her relationship with Diego. They served as a powerful counterpoint to the conventional portrayal of women in art, asserting her individuality and reclaiming her agency in a world often dominated by masculine perspectives.

Frida's independence extended beyond her art. Despite the tumultuous nature of their relationship, she maintained her own social circles and engaged in political activities independent of Diego. Her unwavering commitment to Mexican identity, her involvement in communist circles, and her dedication to social justice demonstrated a commitment to ideals that transcended the boundaries of their marriage. She was a woman with her own convictions, a political consciousness, and a strong sense of purpose that fueled her artistic and personal life.

The challenges of their relationship, including Diego's infidelity and Frida's physical and emotional struggles, served as catalysts for her artistic expression. Her pain, both physical and emotional, became a source of inspiration, fueling her artistic creativity and allowing her to translate her experiences into powerful and evocative works. These works, far from being solely about her relationship with Diego, became a testament to her resilience, her capacity for self-reflection, and her ability to transform adversity into art.

Frida's relationship with Diego was a complex tapestry woven with threads of love, passion, artistic collaboration, and profound personal challenges. It was a relationship that tested the boundaries of conventional marriage and challenged societal expectations of gender roles. Yet, it was through Frida's unwavering strength, her independent spirit, and her artistic voice that she navigated the complexities of their union and emerged as a visionary artist whose impact continues to resonate today. Her legacy serves as a reminder that even in the midst of challenges and complexities, human strength and resilience can triumph, paving the way for self-discovery and artistic expression that transcends the limitations of circumstance.

Chapter 10: The Power of Self-Expression:

Exploring the feminist themes and messages in her work

Frida Kahlo's art transcended the boundaries of mere self-expression, becoming a powerful platform for challenging societal norms and advocating for female empowerment. Throughout her oeuvre, she unflinchingly explored themes of womanhood, sexuality, and self-determination, challenging traditional gender roles and expectations. Her canvases became battlegrounds where she fought for female agency and celebrated the complexities and strengths of the feminine experience.

One of the most striking aspects of Kahlo's feminist message lies in her **self-portraits**. These are not mere depictions of her physical appearance but rather deeply personal explorations of her identity, struggles, and triumphs as a woman. In paintings like **"The Two Fridas"** (1939), she delves into the duality of her own being, showcasing the strength and vulnerability inherent in her identity. The two Fridas, connected by a shared artery, represent different facets of her personality, reflecting her internal conflict and resilience.

Beyond the duality of the self, Kahlo also used her art to challenge traditional representations of femininity. In paintings like **"The Broken Column"** (1944), she embraces a raw and visceral portrayal of her physical pain, refusing to shy away from depicting her body as a site of both vulnerability and strength. This defiance of idealized beauty standards, coupled with her unapologetically **androgynous style** and her bold use of color, further challenged conventional notions of femininity.

Furthermore, Kahlo's work delved into the complexities of female sexuality and its societal constraints. In paintings like **"The Wounded Table"** (1940), she uses a combination of anatomical imagery and symbolic objects to explore the pain of betrayal and the struggle to reclaim one's sexual agency. The juxtaposition of a bloody table, a fetus, and a surgical instrument, alludes to the physical and emotional wounds inflicted by her husband's infidelity, but also to her own defiant strength in reclaiming her body and emotions.

Kahlo's feminist message was further amplified by her political activism. While she was deeply affected by the Mexican Revolution, she was also a vocal supporter of communist ideals, challenging capitalist structures and advocating for social justice. Her paintings often incorporated political symbols and imagery, reflecting her commitment to social change and the fight against oppression. This intersection of feminist and political activism solidified her position as a radical voice for liberation and equality.

In the face of immense personal suffering and societal pressures, Frida Kahlo emerged as a defiant icon of female strength and self-expression. Her art, imbued with feminist themes and messages, continues to resonate with audiences worldwide, inspiring generations to embrace their individuality, challenge norms, and fight for equality. She stands as a testament to the power of art as a tool for social change and a powerful symbol of female agency in a world that often seeks to silence women's voices.

The celebration of female strength, sexuality, and self-determination

While Frida Kahlo's art was undeniably autobiographical, it resonated deeply with a broader audience, particularly women, for its powerful exploration of femininity, sexuality, and self-determination. Kahlo's self-portraits, often filled with vivid colors, symbolic imagery, and unflinching honesty, became a testament to her resilience, her defiant spirit, and her refusal to be defined by societal expectations.

One of the most striking aspects of Kahlo's work is the way she embraced her own sexuality. In a time when women were expected to be demure and modest, Kahlo painted herself with a frankness and sensuality that was both shocking and liberating. From the boldly painted unibrow and mustache to her revealing clothing, she refused to shy away from her physicality. Her self-portraits celebrated the female form in all its complexity and power, challenging the prevailing notions of female beauty and desirability.

Beyond her physical portrayal, Kahlo's paintings often contained symbolic references to female sexuality, fertility, and power. She used flowers, for example, as a recurring motif to symbolize both the beauty and fragility of womanhood. In "The Two Fridas," a poignant double portrait, Kahlo depicts herself as two distinct entities, one connected to a beating heart and the other to a severed artery, highlighting the duality of female experience, strength and vulnerability.

Kahlo's unapologetic expression of her sexuality was not merely about physical attributes; it was a powerful statement about her control over her own body and her refusal to be objectified or silenced. She challenged the patriarchal norms that confined women to domesticity and subservience. In "The Broken Column," she depicted herself as a woman literally broken, yet enduring, symbolizing the crushing weight of societal expectations on women.

Kahlo's work celebrated the strength of women, both physically and emotionally. Despite enduring a lifetime of physical pain, illness, and the emotional turmoil of her relationship with Diego Rivera, Kahlo never allowed these experiences to define her. She refused to be a victim; instead, she used her art to transform her suffering into a source of power and inspiration. She painted with a ferocity that mirrored her indomitable spirit, showcasing her strength in the face of adversity.

Kahlo's commitment to self-determination was evident in every aspect of her life. She was fiercely independent, both in her personal and artistic pursuits. She refused to be defined by her husband's fame or her physical limitations. She chose to live life on her own terms, defying societal expectations and pursuing her own creative vision.

Ultimately, Frida Kahlo's art is a testament to the power of self-expression. By embracing her own sexuality, celebrating her own strength, and refusing to conform to societal norms, she became a symbol of female empowerment. Her work continues to inspire women across generations to embrace their own individuality, fight for their rights, and live life on their own terms.

Challenging societal expectations and traditional gender roles

Frida Kahlo's life and art were a defiant rebellion against the constricting societal norms and expectations placed upon women in her time. In a world where women were expected to conform to traditional roles as wives, mothers, and homemakers, Frida carved her own path, defying conventions and embracing her individuality. Her paintings became a powerful platform for challenging gender stereotypes and celebrating female strength, sexuality, and self-determination.

Frida's **self-portraits** are not mere depictions of her physical appearance but profound explorations of her inner world, her identity, and her defiance against societal expectations. She used her art to reclaim her body, often depicting herself in a way that challenged the idealized feminine beauty standards of her era. Her **unibrow**, which she proudly embraced, became a symbol of her refusal to conform to conventional notions of beauty. She adorned herself with **traditional Mexican clothing** and jewelry, celebrating her cultural heritage and rejecting the Western aesthetic that was dominant in the art world.

Her paintings often depicted her body in a raw and unflinching manner, embracing her physical struggles with pain and illness. In doing so, she broke the taboo surrounding female bodies and sexuality, refusing to shy away from the realities of the female experience. Her self-portraits often featured **anatomical imagery**, **blood**, and **bodily fluids**, exposing the vulnerabilities and complexities of being a woman. This defiance of societal norms shocked and challenged the traditional views on female representation in art.

Beyond the physical, Frida's art also addressed the emotional and psychological realities of being a woman in a patriarchal society. Her paintings explored themes of **love**, **loss**, and **passion**, highlighting the complexities of female desire and relationships. She depicted herself in **powerful** and **confident** poses, often challenging the traditional roles of femininity that confined women to submissive and passive positions.

Frida's relationship with Diego Rivera, a prominent Mexican muralist, further fueled her defiance against societal expectations. Their turbulent and passionate relationship, marked by infidelity and constant challenges, mirrored the complexities of female autonomy and the struggle for power in a patriarchal society. Frida's art often reflected the emotional turmoil of this relationship, revealing the struggles of women to maintain their independence and self-worth within the confines of traditional marriage.

Her paintings became a rallying cry for feminist ideals, long before the rise of the contemporary feminist movement. Frida's unwavering spirit, her refusal to conform to societal expectations, and her celebration of female strength and sexuality resonated with women across generations. She became an icon for women who sought to challenge traditional gender roles and embrace their individuality.

Frida's legacy as a feminist icon continues to inspire and empower women today. Her art serves as a powerful reminder that women have the right to define themselves on their own terms, to celebrate their bodies and sexuality, and to challenge the limitations imposed upon them by society. Her defiant spirit and her bold exploration of female experience continue to resonate in a world where the fight for gender equality remains a constant struggle.

Chapter 11: Finding Strength in Pain:

Overcoming multiple surgeries, illnesses, and the impact of her accidents

Frida Kahlo's life was a tapestry woven with threads of pain and resilience. The bus accident that shattered her young body at age 18 cast a long shadow over her life, but it also fueled the fire of her artistic spirit. This traumatic event left her with a lifetime of physical pain and suffering, requiring countless surgeries and enduring bouts of illness. Yet, she refused to be defined by her limitations, turning her suffering into a source of artistic inspiration.

The accident's immediate aftermath was a nightmare. Her pelvis was crushed, her spine fractured in three places, her right leg shattered, and her foot severely injured. A steel corset was permanently fastened to her body, a constant reminder of her broken frame. The pain was relentless, and the doctors despaired, believing she would never walk again. However, Frida's indomitable spirit refused to surrender. With unwavering determination, she fought for her recovery, enduring excruciating physical therapy and countless surgeries. The ordeal left her with chronic pain, which she often described as a constant companion, a presence that permeated her life and her art.

Despite the physical challenges, Frida's spirit remained unbroken. The accident forced her to confront the fragility of the human body and the inevitability of death. This dark confrontation spurred a new artistic urgency, fueling her self-portraits and shaping her artistic vision. She began to explore themes of pain, suffering, and mortality, rendering the physical and emotional anguish of her experience with raw honesty.

The accident also led to a series of debilitating illnesses. From the beginning, Frida struggled with chronic pain and infections, often confined to her bed. She endured numerous surgeries, some of which left her physically and emotionally scarred. The years after the accident were filled with medical interventions, leaving her body a canvas of scars, bandages, and surgical apparatuses.

One of Frida's most iconic paintings, The Broken Column, serves as a powerful testament to her enduring struggle. The painting depicts her standing with a broken column, a symbol of her own shattered body, piercing her through the heart. Her body is contorted with pain, a stark portrayal of the physical suffering she endured. Yet, within the imagery of brokenness, there is a remarkable sense of strength and defiance. Frida refuses to be defined by her pain; instead, she embraces it as a part of her identity, a source of inspiration, and a catalyst for her artistic expression.

Despite the relentless onslaught of physical and emotional pain, Frida's art thrived. The accident became a turning point in her artistic journey, pushing her to explore deeper into the realm of self-expression. She began to use her art as a means of healing, finding solace in the act of creation. Her self-portraits became a way of processing her pain, documenting her journey, and confronting her mortality.

In her art, Frida transformed her suffering into a visual language of resilience. She celebrated the fragility and strength of the human body, highlighting the power of the human spirit to endure even in the face of unimaginable hardship. She embraced her pain not as a weakness, but as a source of strength, using it to create art that would inspire generations to come.

Frida's life was a testament to the human capacity for resilience. She refused to be defined by her physical limitations, turning her suffering into a source of artistic creation. Her paintings are a poignant reminder of the enduring power of the human spirit, a testament to the strength found in vulnerability, and a celebration of the transformative power of art.

The power of art as a coping mechanism and emotional outlet

Frida Kahlo's life was a tapestry woven with threads of pain, resilience, and the unwavering pursuit of self-expression. Throughout her tumultuous journey, marked by chronic illness, debilitating injuries, and emotional turmoil, she found solace and strength in the transformative power of art. Art became her sanctuary, a refuge where she could confront her inner demons, grapple with the complexities of her existence, and ultimately, reclaim her own narrative.

From a young age, Kahlo's artistic inclinations served as a conduit for navigating the world. She was drawn to vivid colors, symbolic imagery, and the power of visual storytelling. This innate talent proved invaluable during her early years, as she coped with the profound psychological impact of a severe bus accident in 1925. The accident left her with lasting physical pain and emotional scars, prompting a deep introspection that would forever shape her artistic vision.

Confined to bed for extended periods, Kahlo found herself grappling with the limitations of her physical body and the fragility of human existence. The intense physical and emotional pain she endured became the fuel for her artistic expression, transforming suffering into raw, unflinching self-portraits that resonated with honesty and vulnerability. Her iconic self-portraits, often depicting her entangled with medical apparatuses, served as powerful visual testaments to her resilience, challenging conventional notions of beauty and femininity. Through her art, she found a way to transcend physical limitations, embracing her pain and transforming it into a source of artistic inspiration.

As Kahlo's physical and emotional well-being fluctuated throughout her life, her art provided a consistent outlet for processing her experiences. She often turned to surrealism, a movement that embraced the subconscious mind and the merging of dreams and reality. This artistic style allowed her to explore the complexities of her own psyche, delving into themes of identity, sexuality, and the existential nature of life and death. Her paintings became a canvas for confronting her fears, desires, and anxieties, offering a window into the depths of her soul.

Beyond her personal struggles, Kahlo's art served as a platform for political and social commentary. She channeled her experiences of pain, suffering, and resilience into a powerful critique of societal norms, challenging traditional gender roles and advocating for female empowerment. Through her bold self-portraits and evocative imagery, she embraced her unconventional identity, celebrating female strength, sexuality, and self-determination. Her art became a vehicle for challenging societal expectations, promoting a greater understanding of the female experience, and igniting conversations around feminist ideals.

The enduring power of Frida Kahlo's art lies in its ability to connect with universal human experiences. Her unflinching honesty, vulnerability, and unwavering spirit inspire generations of artists, activists, and individuals who seek to find strength and solace amidst life's challenges. By transforming her pain into art, she created a legacy of resilience, empowerment, and the transformative power of self-expression. Her art serves as a testament to the enduring strength of the human spirit and the ability to find beauty and meaning even in the darkest of times.

Finding solace and strength in her creativity and self-expression

Throughout her life, Frida Kahlo faced a relentless onslaught of physical and emotional challenges. From the devastating bus accident that shattered her body and spirit to the constant pain that plagued her existence, she found herself navigating a landscape of suffering that would have overwhelmed most individuals. Yet, Frida possessed an indomitable spirit and an unwavering determination to not only survive but to thrive in the face of adversity. It was within the realm of her art, within the act of creation, that she discovered a sanctuary, a powerful outlet to confront her pain, and ultimately, a source of resilience that propelled her forward.

Her art became a conduit for processing her pain, transforming it into a visual language that reflected the complexities of her inner world. The canvases she adorned with vibrant colors and intricate details served as a mirror to her soul, revealing the profound impact of her suffering on her identity, her relationships, and her perception of the world. Through the act of painting, she confronted the physical and emotional wounds that marked her existence, transforming them into potent symbols of her strength and resilience.

Frida's iconic self-portraits stand as testament to her ability to confront her pain and find meaning in suffering. These intimate portraits are not merely representations of her physical appearance but delve deep into the psychological landscapes of her being. They reveal the raw vulnerability of her spirit, the physical limitations imposed upon her body, and the intense emotional struggles she endured. Yet, within these portraits, a powerful undercurrent of defiance and self-affirmation emerges. Frida refused to shy away from her pain, choosing instead to embrace it, to paint it onto the canvas, and to transform it into a source of artistic expression.

In paintings like *The Broken Column*, she uses the imagery of a fractured column to represent her broken body, a symbol of the physical limitations she faced. The image of a metal corset binding her body speaks to the restrictive nature of her physical condition, but also to the constraints imposed on her by societal expectations. Her painting *Henry Ford Hospital*, a dreamlike depiction of her hospitalization and miscarriage, reveals the profound impact of her physical pain on her emotional well-being. Yet, in the midst of these raw and poignant images, a flicker of hope, a testament to her resilience, shines through.

Frida's art was not simply a reflection of her pain but an act of rebellion against it. She refused to be defined by her suffering; instead, she transformed it into a source of creative energy, a driving force that propelled her artistic vision. Through the act of creation, she found a way to reclaim her agency, to assert her control over her narrative, and to channel her pain into a powerful testament to her strength and resilience.

The very act of painting, of bringing her inner world to life on the canvas, became an act of defiance. It was a way of asserting her presence, her voice, her identity in the face of a world that sought to define her by her physical limitations. It was a testament to the power of the human spirit to overcome adversity, to find solace and strength in the creative act, and to transform suffering into a source of art and inspiration.

For Frida, art was not merely a form of expression but a vital lifeline. It was a means of survival, a way of making sense of the chaos of her existence, and a powerful tool for reclaiming her agency in a world that sought to define her by her pain. It was within the creative process, within the act of transforming her pain into art, that she found the strength to overcome adversity, to celebrate her individuality, and to leave behind a legacy that would inspire generations to come.

Chapter 12: Beyond the Physical:

Frida's engagement with spiritualism and her exploration of the afterlife

Throughout her life, Frida Kahlo grappled with profound existential questions, wrestling not only with the physical pain of her injuries but also with the deeper anxieties about mortality and the unknown that lay beyond. While her art often reflected her physical struggles and personal tribulations, it also delved into the realm of spirituality and the mystical, revealing a deep fascination with the afterlife.

Frida's exploration of spiritualism was influenced by a number of factors, including her upbringing in a family steeped in Mexican traditions and her exposure to indigenous beliefs. Mexico boasts a rich and complex tapestry of spiritual practices, including folk magic, ancient rituals, and a strong belief in the interconnectedness of life and death. Frida's mother, Matilde Calderón, played a significant role in nurturing her daughter's fascination with the mystical, introducing her to the world of traditional

Mexican healing practices, where the boundaries between the physical and spiritual were often blurred.

Frida's engagement with spiritualism became more pronounced in the later years of her life, when she was battling chronic pain and facing the limitations of her physical body. The bus accident, which had shattered her physical form and left her with excruciating pain, served as a catalyst for her exploration of the intangible. She began to seek solace in alternative healing practices, including homeopathic remedies and spiritual consultations, and her art increasingly reflected her interest in the afterlife, the nature of the soul, and the connection between the living and the dead.

Frida's fascination with death and rebirth was deeply intertwined with her exploration of the spiritual realm. Her paintings frequently feature imagery related to death, such as skulls, skeletons, and decaying bodies, yet these images are not depicted in a morbid or macabre way. Instead, they symbolize the cycle of life and death, the inevitability of mortality, and the possibility of transcendence beyond the physical realm.

One of Frida's most iconic paintings, **The Two Fridas**, (1939) provides a powerful example of her engagement with spiritualism. The painting depicts two versions of Frida, joined by a single artery, representing the duality of her spirit and the interconnectedness of her physical and spiritual selves. The Frida on the left, dressed in a traditional Mexican **Tehuana** dress, holds a heart exposed for all to see, while the Frida on the right, in a white medical gown, reveals a dissected heart. This juxtaposition symbolizes the struggle between her Mexican identity and her European heritage, between her physical and spiritual selves, and between the beauty and pain of existence. It also reflects Frida's belief in the enduring nature of the soul, even in the face of death.

Frida's artistic exploration of death and spirituality was often intertwined with her exploration of Mexican culture and tradition. Her paintings frequently incorporated elements of Mexican folklore, such as **Day of the Dead** imagery and Aztec symbolism. These elements allowed Frida to express her deep connection to her cultural roots and her belief in the cyclical nature of life and death.

The influence of indigenous Mexican spiritual beliefs, such as the belief in the interconnectedness of life and death and the importance of ancestors, is evident in Frida's art. Her paintings frequently feature images of pre-Hispanic deities and symbolism, such as the **Coatlicue**, a powerful Aztec goddess associated with the Earth, motherhood, and creation. These images speak to Frida's belief in a spiritual realm that transcends the physical and her connection to the ancient wisdom of her ancestors.

Frida's engagement with spiritualism was not just a reflection of her personal beliefs but also a testament to her unique artistic vision. She transcended the boundaries of traditional art forms, embracing the spiritual and mystical dimensions of human existence. Her paintings often reflected her own personal struggles with pain and suffering, but they also offered a glimpse into a deeper understanding of the human condition, the interconnectedness of life and death, and the enduring nature of the soul. Her art continues to inspire and provoke, reminding us of the power of art to transcend the limitations of the physical realm and to explore the mysteries of the universe.

The use of symbolism and imagery related to death and rebirth

Frida Kahlo's art is a testament to her enduring spirit and her deep engagement with themes of life, death, and the cyclical nature of existence. She faced immense physical and emotional challenges, and her art reflects her unique perspective on mortality, suffering, and the transformative power of the human spirit. Within her works, a compelling narrative unfolds, one where death and rebirth interweave, creating a powerful symbolism that resonates with viewers even today.

One of the most striking examples of this symbolism is found in her iconic self-portrait, ***"The Two Fridas"*** (1939). This painting depicts two versions of Frida, both connected by a single artery that pumps blood from one heart to the other. The Frida on the left, dressed in a traditional Tehuana gown, represents her Mexican identity and her connection to her indigenous roots. The other Frida, on the right, is dressed in a European-style gown, symbolizing her Western influences and her struggle with the duality of her cultural heritage. The artery connecting them represents the shared blood that unites them, but it is also a symbol of the pain and trauma that Frida experienced, as it is torn apart and exposed. The severed artery signifies the deep wounds she carried, both physical and emotional, as a result of her bus accident.

This painting's central theme is the intertwined nature of life and death, with Frida's heart at the center of it all. The severed artery visually represents her pain and trauma, yet it also serves as a bridge between the two Fridas, highlighting the strength she found in embracing her dual nature. The image of the torn heart, with its raw and exposed vulnerability, acts as a powerful symbol of Frida's journey through pain and suffering, ultimately emerging as a resilient and defiant force. This image transcends simple death and rebirth; it signifies a profound transformation, a symbolic resurrection of her spirit and her artistic vision.

The imagery of *"The Two Fridas"* foreshadows Frida's later works, where she further explores themes of mortality and rebirth, often using the human body as a vessel for symbolic representation. In her self-portrait *"The Broken Column"* (1944), Frida portrays herself as a shattered column, its broken parts held together by nails, symbolizing the pain and suffering she endured throughout her life. The image of the nails, piercing her flesh and anchoring her together, alludes to her physical injuries but also serves as a symbol of her resilience and her ability to endure and rise above her pain. The *broken column*, a symbol of strength and endurance, represents the physical and emotional scars that marked Frida's life, yet it also represents her tenacious spirit and her refusal to be broken by her suffering.

Similarly, in her self-portrait *"Self-Portrait with Thorn Necklace and Hummingbird"* (1940), Frida depicts herself adorned with a necklace of thorns, piercing her flesh. The image is both painful and beautiful, evoking a sense of vulnerability and resilience. The hummingbird, a symbol of freedom and transformation, hovers above the thorns, suggesting that even in the midst of pain and suffering, there is the possibility of healing and rebirth. The thorns, representing her pain and suffering, are juxtaposed against the hummingbird, a symbol of freedom and renewal, highlighting the duality of life and death, pain and beauty, within Frida's experience.

Frida Kahlo's art is replete with symbolic imagery that reflects her deep understanding of the interconnectedness of life and death. She embraces the pain and suffering she endured, finding strength and beauty in the face of adversity. Her works are not simply depictions of her struggles but powerful explorations of the human condition, filled with symbols of resilience, transformation, and the enduring power of the human spirit.

The influence of indigenous Mexican spiritual beliefs on her work

Frida Kahlo's art was deeply intertwined with her Mexican heritage, and her indigenous roots played a significant role in shaping her artistic vision and worldview. Mexico's rich tapestry of pre-Columbian cultures, with their vibrant myths, rituals, and spiritual beliefs, served as a constant source of inspiration for her. Kahlo's paintings often incorporated elements of Aztec, Maya, and other indigenous traditions, reflecting a profound connection to her ancestral past and a reverence for the spiritual forces that permeated her surroundings.

One prominent aspect of indigenous Mexican spirituality that deeply resonated with Kahlo was the concept of *dualism*, the belief in the interconnectedness of opposites, such as life and death, light and darkness, masculine and feminine. This duality is evident in her self-portraits, where she often depicted herself alongside symbols of both life and death, such as flowers and skulls. The juxtaposition of these elements underscored her embrace of the cyclical nature of life and her acceptance of mortality as an integral part of the human experience.

Another key influence was the indigenous reverence for *nature* and its powerful symbolism. Kahlo's paintings are often adorned with vibrant flora and fauna, reflecting the rich biodiversity of Mexico. The flowers she depicted, particularly marigolds, held deep significance in indigenous traditions as symbols of death and remembrance, but also of resilience and renewal. Kahlo's use of flowers in her self-portraits, often placed around her head or spilling from her body, conveyed a complex interplay between life, death, and the cyclical nature of existence. She imbued these natural elements with personal meaning, using them to explore themes of suffering, healing, and the enduring power of the human spirit.

Her artistic exploration of ***indigenous deities***, such as the Aztec goddess Coatlicue, is another testament to her fascination with Mexican mythology and spirituality. Coatlicue, a powerful deity associated with creation and destruction, resonated with Kahlo's personal struggle with pain and mortality. In her painting "The Two Fridas," Coatlicue's iconic imagery is woven into the canvas, hinting at the complex interplay of life and death, the feminine archetype, and Kahlo's own struggle with identity. By incorporating these deities into her work, Kahlo not only paid homage to her cultural heritage but also drew upon their power to explore her own personal mythology and wrestle with existential questions.

Frida Kahlo's engagement with indigenous Mexican spiritual beliefs extended beyond her visual art. Her deep connection to her roots was also reflected in her personal life. She often wore traditional Mexican clothing, celebrated indigenous holidays, and was deeply interested in ancient Mayan rituals and ceremonies. This personal connection to her cultural heritage undoubtedly informed her artistic vision and contributed to the profound depth and meaning that infused her work.

Kahlo's embrace of indigenous Mexican spiritual beliefs was not simply a decorative element in her art; it was a fundamental aspect of her identity and a source of strength and inspiration. By incorporating these beliefs into her self-portraits and other paintings, she transcended the boundaries of traditional art, creating a unique and powerful visual language that resonated with the complexities of human existence, the cyclical nature of life and death, and the enduring power of the human spirit.

Part IV: Legacy and Impact

Chapter 13: The Rise of a Feminist Icon:

The enduring legacy of Frida Kahlo and her influence on the feminist movement

Frida Kahlo's legacy extends far beyond her captivating self-portraits and vibrant palette. She is celebrated not only as a master artist but also as a powerful icon of feminism, inspiring generations with her unwavering spirit, raw vulnerability, and defiant embrace of individuality. Her life and work serve as a testament to the strength and resilience of women, challenging societal norms and advocating for female agency.

Kahlo's journey was marked by immense pain and adversity, yet she never relinquished her feminist ideals. Despite the patriarchal society she navigated, she refused to conform to societal expectations. From her unyielding spirit to her unapologetic self-expression, Kahlo embodied a feminist ethos, demonstrating that women could be both powerful and vulnerable, sensual and intelligent, defiant and compassionate.

Her art, often infused with feminist undertones, challenged traditional notions of femininity. Her self-portraits, meticulously crafted with intense emotion and vibrant symbolism, transcended mere depictions of the self. They became powerful pronouncements of female agency, challenging the objectification and control that women often faced. In her iconic self-portrait "The Two Fridas," Kahlo depicts two versions of herself, one connected to her Mexican heritage and the other to her European upbringing, symbolizing the multifaceted nature of womanhood and the complexities of identity.

Kahlo's exploration of pain and suffering, often linked to her physical and emotional struggles, became a powerful metaphor for female resilience. Her art, far from being merely biographical, resonated with women who understood the physical and emotional burdens they carried. Her feminist perspective challenged the societal silencing of women's experiences, particularly those related to pain, childbirth, and mental health. Her work gave voice to the often-unacknowledged struggles of women, allowing them to see their own pain reflected in her art, fostering a sense of solidarity and understanding.

Kahlo's relationship with Diego Rivera, a prominent muralist and her husband, added another layer to her feminist identity. The complexities of their relationship, marked by passion, infidelity, and mutual respect, offered a glimpse into the struggles of women within patriarchal relationships. Despite Rivera's fame and dominance, Kahlo maintained her artistic independence and voice, refusing to be defined solely by her relationship with a man. She challenged the notion that women were simply wives or muses, showcasing her own strength and artistic prowess.

While Kahlo's feminist message was not explicitly stated, it resonated deeply with women who saw themselves reflected in her struggle and defiance. Her celebration of female sexuality, often expressed through her vibrant attire, symbolic imagery, and unconventional beauty, challenged traditional notions of feminine modesty. Her unflinching gaze, the powerful presence she embodied in her self-portraits, resonated with a growing feminist movement that sought to reclaim women's agency and visibility.

Kahlo's influence on the feminist movement goes beyond her artistic achievements. Her life, characterized by resilience, defiance, and a commitment to self-expression, continues to inspire women worldwide. She reminds us that women can be powerful, vulnerable, and multifaceted, and that our journeys are uniquely our own. Kahlo's enduring legacy as a feminist icon lies in her ability to empower women, celebrate their individuality, and challenge the limitations imposed by a patriarchal society. Her art remains a powerful reminder that women's voices deserve to be heard, their experiences acknowledged, and their struggles celebrated. Through her legacy, Kahlo continues to inspire a new generation of women to embrace their own power and redefine what it means to be a woman in the world.

The celebration of female power, resilience, and self-empowerment

Frida Kahlo's life and art were a defiant testament to the power of the human spirit, particularly the spirit of a woman navigating a world often defined by male dominance. Her story, marked by physical and emotional hardship, served as a platform for celebrating the resilience and self-empowerment that she embodied. This chapter delves into how Kahlo's work challenged conventional gender roles, championed female strength, and inspired generations of women to embrace their authentic selves.

Kahlo's self-portraits, often painted with unflinching honesty, became a visual manifesto of female agency. She depicted herself with a boldness that defied the traditional, often idealized portrayals of women in art. Her unibrow, a defining feature, was not merely a physical trait but a symbol of her resistance to the pressures of societal beauty standards. She embraced her unique appearance, transforming it into a powerful statement of individuality and self-acceptance.

Beyond physical features, Kahlo's paintings explored the multifaceted nature of femininity. She did not shy away from depicting female sexuality, often portraying herself in a provocative and sensual manner, challenging the notion of female modesty and sexual repression. Her self-portraits, like "*The Two Fridas*," showcased the complexity of female identity, showcasing both vulnerability and strength. These works served as a powerful reminder of the unbreakable spirit of women, capable of experiencing a full spectrum of emotions and desires.

Kahlo's engagement with Mexican folk art further underlined her celebration of female power. She incorporated traditional textiles, clothing, and cultural motifs into her work, drawing on the legacy of strong, independent women in Mexican culture. Her paintings, like "*The Broken Column*," depict a woman enduring immense pain but ultimately standing firm, a testament to the strength found in facing adversity head-on.

While Kahlo's art directly addressed themes of feminine strength, her life itself was a powerful illustration of resilience. She endured numerous surgeries, chronic pain, and emotional turmoil, yet she channeled her struggles into her art, using it as a form of empowerment. She refused to let her physical limitations define her, instead using her art to explore the complexities of her own experience and, in doing so, inspire others to do the same.

Kahlo's legacy extends far beyond the realm of art. Her life and work became a rallying cry for the feminist movement, inspiring generations of women to embrace their individuality, challenge societal expectations, and celebrate their power. Her bold self-expression and unwavering commitment to her own vision resonated with a global audience, serving as a powerful reminder of the strength and resilience that lies within each woman.

Her enduring impact on art, fashion, and popular culture

Frida Kahlo's influence extends far beyond the realm of art, permeating fashion, popular culture, and the very fabric of modern consciousness. Her iconic self-portraits, infused with vibrant colors, bold imagery, and raw emotional honesty, have become symbols of female strength, resilience, and self-expression. Her unique style, a fusion of Mexican folk art, Surrealism, and personal symbolism, has captivated generations, inspiring artists, designers, and individuals alike.

A Fashion Icon:

Frida Kahlo's bold, androgynous fashion sense has become a defining element of her persona. Her signature unibrow, colorful embroidered dresses, and traditional Mexican clothing have been endlessly imitated and reinterpreted by fashion designers and trendsetters. Her style, a powerful statement of cultural pride, individual expression, and defiance of traditional beauty standards, continues to inspire designers to explore themes of femininity, identity, and cultural appropriation.

From high-end fashion houses to independent designers, Frida Kahlo's influence is evident in print patterns, embroidery, jewelry, and accessories. Her image has graced countless fashion campaigns, magazine covers, and runway shows, becoming a potent symbol of feminine power, artistic brilliance, and cultural iconoclasm.

Art's Everlasting Muse:

Beyond fashion, Frida Kahlo's impact on art has been profound and lasting. Her unique artistic voice, a blend of realism, surrealism, and self-exploration, challenged conventional notions of beauty and redefined the role of the artist as a chronicler of personal struggles and societal realities. Her fearless portrayal of pain, suffering, and mortality paved the way for a new era of vulnerability and authenticity in artistic expression.

Contemporary artists continue to draw inspiration from Frida Kahlo's legacy, exploring themes of identity, gender, and cultural representation through their own unique lens. Her impact is felt in a multitude of art forms, from painting and sculpture to photography, film, and performance art. Her work serves as a constant reminder of the power of art to transform personal experiences into universal truths and to challenge societal norms.

A Global Icon:

Frida Kahlo's impact extends far beyond the art world, reaching into popular culture and the collective consciousness of a global audience. Her image has become a ubiquitous symbol of rebellion, strength, and artistic expression. She has been featured in countless books, films, documentaries, and music videos, solidifying her status as a cultural icon.

Her legacy continues to inspire and empower individuals worldwide. Her story of overcoming adversity, embracing individuality, and defying societal expectations resonates with people from all walks of life. Her enduring impact serves as a testament to the power of artistic expression, cultural diversity, and personal resilience.

Chapter 14: The Art of Frida Kahlo:

Analysis of her most iconic paintings and their meanings

Frida Kahlo's artistic output, though relatively small in number, is immensely powerful and impactful. Her paintings, often autobiographical and intensely personal, delve into themes of pain, identity, Mexican culture, and the complexities of her life. This chapter will analyze some of her most iconic works, exploring the layers of meaning embedded within their vivid imagery and symbolism.

The Two Fridas (1939)

One of Kahlo's most famous and complex paintings, The Two Fridas portrays two versions of herself, connected by a single artery. The Frida on the left, dressed in traditional Tehuana clothing, represents her Mexican identity and her connection to her roots. The Frida on the right, clad in a European-style gown, symbolizes her more Westernized side and her aspirations for love and connection. The shared artery represents the intertwined nature of her identity, as well as the pain and heartbreak she experienced in her relationship with Diego Rivera. This dual depiction also reflects her exploration of her own femininity and her struggle to reconcile her Mexican heritage with her Western upbringing.

The Broken Column (1944)

The Broken Column is a powerful and visceral expression of Kahlo's physical and emotional pain. It depicts her standing with a broken column in place of her spine, representing the devastating impact of her bus accident. Her body is pierced with nails, symbolizing the constant suffering she endured. A bloody tear streams down her face, a poignant symbol of her pain and vulnerability. The background features a melancholic landscape, reflecting the bleakness of her emotional state. This painting serves as a stark reminder of Kahlo's resilience in the face of immense suffering, her determination to endure the pain and continue to create art.

Henry Ford Hospital (1932)

Henry Ford Hospital is a deeply personal and symbolic work that explores Kahlo's experience with miscarriage and the subsequent emotional and physical pain. The painting features a stark, clinical setting, a hospital bed with medical equipment, and a fetus floating in a dark, chaotic space. A blood vessel, connected to Kahlo's heart and the fetus, represents the physical and emotional connection she felt to her lost child. The juxtaposition of the clinical setting and the ethereal, symbolic imagery highlights the contrast between the medical reality of her situation and the profound emotional impact of her loss. The painting serves as a powerful testament to the devastating experience of miscarriage and the emotional complexities of motherhood.

Self-Portrait with Thorn Necklace and Hummingbird (1940)

In Self-Portrait with Thorn Necklace and Hummingbird, Kahlo explores themes of love, pain, and resilience. She portrays herself with a thorn necklace, symbolizing the pain and anguish of her relationship with Diego Rivera. A hummingbird, representing love and freedom, hovers above her, suggesting the possibility of escape from the pain. The juxtaposition of the thorn necklace and the hummingbird highlights the complex duality of her love for Rivera, both beautiful and painful. The painting also reflects Kahlo's deep connection to nature and her ability to find beauty amidst suffering.

The Wounded Table (1940)

The Wounded Table is a surreal and symbolic representation of Kahlo's pain and her struggle to cope with her physical and emotional wounds. The table, a symbol of nourishment and sustenance, is depicted with a gaping wound, bleeding and broken. A fragmented anatomical heart, representing her emotional pain, lies upon the table. The surrounding objects, such as a broken surgical instrument and a bleeding flower, all contribute to the overall sense of fragmentation and despair. This painting underscores the profound impact of Kahlo's physical and emotional injuries on her life and her artistic practice.

Self-Portrait with Monkey (1938)

Self-Portrait with Monkey is a striking image that showcases Kahlo's playful and rebellious spirit. She depicts herself with a pet monkey, a symbol of her independence and her ability to defy expectations. The monkey, a playful and intelligent creature, suggests her connection to nature and her unconventional approach to life. The backdrop of the painting features a lush, tropical landscape, reflecting her deep connection to Mexico and its natural beauty. The painting embodies Kahlo's unique spirit, her ability to find joy and laughter amidst suffering, and her refusal to be defined by societal norms.

Self-Portrait with Thorn Necklace and Hummingbird (1940)

This painting is another exploration of love, pain, and resilience. The thorn necklace, representing the pain of her relationship with Diego Rivera, is juxtaposed with the hummingbird, symbolizing love and freedom. The painting shows Kahlo's resilience and ability to find beauty amidst suffering.

Through her iconic paintings, Frida Kahlo delved into the depths of her own experiences, offering a glimpse into the complexities of her life and artistic journey. Her works are a testament to her resilience, her passion for life, and her unwavering spirit. By exploring her most famous works, we gain a deeper understanding of her artistic vision and her enduring legacy as a feminist icon and one of the most important artists of the 20th century.

The evolution of her style and artistic techniques

Frida Kahlo's artistic journey was one of constant evolution, reflecting her own personal struggles, political awakening, and deep connection to her Mexican heritage. Her style, while often categorized as surrealism, transcended mere artistic movements, becoming a unique and powerful expression of her inner world and lived experiences. It was a style that embraced the raw, the visceral, and the intensely personal, transforming pain and suffering into vibrant, symbolic works of art.

Early Explorations: Finding Her Voice

Frida Kahlo's early artistic explorations were marked by a desire to capture the complexities of her own identity. She began by studying the techniques of her father, Guillermo Kahlo, a renowned photographer. He instilled in her a keen eye for detail and a passion for capturing the essence of reality. However, Frida's artistic ambitions soon diverged from his photographic approach. She felt compelled to express herself in a more personal and expressive manner, one that transcended the limitations of mere representation.

Her early works often depicted scenes of daily life, incorporating elements of Mexican folklore and indigenous traditions. These early paintings, while technically proficient, were still finding their unique voice. It was in the wake of her devastating bus accident that Frida Kahlo's artistic style began to truly take shape.

Pain and Symbolism: A New Language of Expression

The accident left Frida Kahlo with severe injuries and chronic pain, a constant reminder of her fragility. This profound experience deeply affected her art, transforming it into a powerful exploration of pain, suffering, and mortality. It was during this period that her iconic style, characterized by vivid imagery, symbolism, and surrealism, emerged.

Her self-portraits became a central focus of her work, serving as a canvas for her internal struggles. In these portraits, Frida Kahlo explored her physical and emotional wounds, often juxtaposing anatomical imagery with elements of Mexican folklore and indigenous traditions. For example, in "The Broken Column" (1944), Frida Kahlo depicted herself as a broken column, physically and emotionally, with a metal rod representing the pain that permeated her being.

Surrealism and the Subconscious: Merging Reality and Fantasy

While Frida Kahlo's art was often associated with Surrealism, her approach differed from the European Surrealist movement. She didn't focus on the purely dreamlike or fantastical, but rather on the merging of reality and fantasy. She sought to explore the depths of her own subconscious, drawing upon her personal experiences, dreams, and cultural heritage to create a unique and powerful visual language.

In works like "The Two Fridas" (1939), Frida Kahlo explored the duality of her identity, portraying two versions of herself – one connected to her Mexican heritage and the other representing the European influences of her upbringing. These two Fridas are connected by a single artery, highlighting the intertwining of her personal and cultural identities.

Mexican Identity: A Tapestry of Tradition and Modernity

Frida Kahlo's art was deeply rooted in her Mexican heritage. She celebrated Mexican culture, identity, and indigenous traditions through her use of vivid colors, traditional clothing, textiles, and flora. She incorporated these elements into her paintings as a testament to her national pride and a recognition of the strength and resilience of her people.

In "The Wounded Deer" (1940), Frida Kahlo used the imagery of a wounded deer to symbolize her own pain and suffering, but also to represent the vulnerability of her nation, Mexico. The deer is adorned with traditional Mexican clothing, highlighting the connection between her personal experiences and the cultural identity of her country.

Evolution of Technique: From Realism to Surrealism

Frida Kahlo's artistic techniques also underwent a significant evolution, reflecting her growth as an artist and the deepening of her personal and artistic vision. Initially, her work was grounded in realism, inspired by the techniques of her father, the photographer.

As she embraced surrealism, her techniques became more experimental and expressive. She used vibrant colors, bold lines, and intricate details to create a heightened sense of reality. Her brushstrokes became more confident and decisive, conveying the raw emotion and visceral nature of her experiences. She often used collage, creating a layered and textured surface that further emphasized the depth and complexity of her work.

From Pain to Power: A Legacy of Resilience

Frida Kahlo's artistic style and techniques evolved over time, mirroring her personal journey of resilience and self-discovery. Her art became a powerful testament to the human spirit's ability to overcome adversity and to find meaning and beauty even in the face of profound pain. Her style, while deeply personal, resonated with audiences worldwide, inspiring generations of artists, activists, and individuals to embrace their own unique identities and to celebrate the power of self-expression.

Her lasting impact on the art world and the development of surrealism

Frida Kahlo's influence on the art world, particularly on the development of surrealism, is undeniable and multifaceted. While she never explicitly identified as a surrealist, her art shared many core tenets of the movement, particularly its exploration of the subconscious, dreams, and the blurring of reality and fantasy. Her unique style, characterized by vibrant colors, symbolic imagery, and raw emotional honesty, resonated with surrealists and contributed to the movement's evolution beyond its European roots.

Kahlo's engagement with surrealism stemmed from her personal experiences and her artistic vision. Her paintings, often autobiographical, delved into her physical and emotional struggles, her tumultuous relationship with Diego Rivera, and her deep connection to Mexican culture and identity. Her use of imagery, particularly self-portraits, served as a window into her inner world, her dreams, and her subconscious. This exploration of the unconscious mind, a hallmark of surrealism, resonated with the movement's core principles.

Kahlo's artistic practice was often a response to her physical and emotional pain. Her bus accident, which left her with lifelong injuries, became a central theme in her art. She used anatomical imagery, blood, and bodily fluids to depict the vulnerability and fragility of the human body. This visceral approach, while often shocking, resonated with surrealism's embrace of the grotesque and the unconventional. It pushed the boundaries of traditional art and challenged societal norms, reflecting a key aspect of the surrealist movement.

While Kahlo's art embraced surrealism's exploration of dreams and the subconscious, it also diverged in key ways. Unlike many European surrealists, who often focused on abstract concepts and dreamlike imagery, Kahlo's art was deeply rooted in her personal experiences and her Mexican heritage. Her paintings often incorporated traditional Mexican clothing, textiles, and flora, blending surrealist elements with a distinctly national identity. This fusion of surrealism with Mexican folklore and cultural motifs contributed to the movement's global reach and its ability to transcend geographical boundaries.

Kahlo's impact on the development of surrealism extended beyond her individual style. Her work challenged the movement's predominantly male perspective, providing a new lens for understanding the female experience. Her self-portraits, often exploring themes of femininity, sexuality, and self-determination, contributed to the feminist discourse within surrealism. This inclusion of female voices and perspectives broadened the movement's scope and enriched its aesthetic and intellectual depth.

Beyond its artistic impact, Kahlo's influence extended to the cultural landscape. Her work became a symbol of resilience, rebellion, and self-expression, particularly for women. Her bold, colorful style and her unflinching honesty resonated with a generation of artists, writers, and activists, inspiring them to embrace their individuality and challenge societal norms. Her legacy transcended the realm of art, becoming a cultural touchstone for generations to come.

In conclusion, Frida Kahlo's influence on the art world, particularly on the development of surrealism, was profound and multifaceted. Her unique style, her exploration of the subconscious, her embrace of the grotesque, and her infusion of Mexican culture into surrealist principles all contributed to the movement's evolution and its global reach. Beyond its artistic impact, Kahlo's legacy as a symbol of female empowerment, resilience, and self-expression continues to inspire artists and activists around the world.

Chapter 15: Frida Kahlo: A Global Icon:

The international recognition and cultural impact of her art

Frida Kahlo's rise to international acclaim is a testament to the enduring power of her art. While her work initially found its footing within the Mexican art scene, its impact transcended geographical boundaries, resonating with audiences worldwide. This global recognition stems from a confluence of factors, including her unique artistic style, her powerful themes of identity, pain, and resilience, and the way she embodied the spirit of Mexican culture and feminism.

In the post-World War II era, as the world began to embrace a spirit of cultural exchange and artistic exploration, Kahlo's work found its way into international exhibitions. Her self-portraits, with their unflinching honesty and raw emotional intensity, captivated audiences across continents. Her use of vibrant colors, bold imagery, and symbolic elements, often drawn from Mexican folklore and indigenous traditions, spoke to a universal human experience that transcended cultural differences.

The international recognition of Kahlo's art was further fueled by the growing interest in surrealism during the latter half of the 20th century. Her work, with its dreamlike quality, its merging of reality and fantasy, and its exploration of the subconscious, resonated with the tenets of surrealism, while simultaneously forging its own distinct path. Kahlo's surrealism, however, was deeply personal, rooted in her own experiences of pain, suffering, and the complexities of human emotions.

Furthermore, Kahlo's work resonated deeply with the burgeoning feminist movement of the 1960s and 1970s. Her self-portraits, which often depicted her as strong, independent, and unapologetically feminine, became a symbol of female empowerment and a challenge to traditional gender roles. Her celebration of female sexuality, her exploration of the female body and its vulnerabilities, and her defiant spirit resonated with a generation seeking to redefine notions of womanhood.

The international recognition of Kahlo's art was also significantly amplified by the role of her legacy. After her death in 1954, her work continued to gain momentum, becoming a focal point of exhibitions and retrospectives across the globe. The establishment of the Frida Kahlo Museum, housed in her former home, "La Casa Azul," in Coyoacán, Mexico, became a pilgrimage site for art enthusiasts from all over the world. The museum, a vibrant celebration of Kahlo's life and artistic legacy, further solidified her status as a global icon.

Today, Frida Kahlo's art continues to inspire and resonate with audiences worldwide. Her iconic self-portraits, her unflinching honesty, her celebration of Mexican culture, and her powerful themes of identity and resilience have made her a global icon. Her influence can be seen in countless artistic endeavors, from fashion and photography to music and literature. Her work has inspired countless artists, writers, and musicians, transcending the boundaries of art and culture to become a universal language of human experience.

Frida Kahlo's impact extends beyond the realm of art. Her image has become a symbol of cultural identity, feminism, and personal strength. Her life and work have inspired countless people to embrace their uniqueness, challenge societal norms, and celebrate their own personal journeys. Her story continues to resonate with a global audience, reminding us of the power of art to transcend boundaries and inspire hope, resilience, and the celebration of individuality.

Her presence in museums, exhibitions, and popular culture

Frida Kahlo's art has transcended the boundaries of time and space, becoming a ubiquitous symbol of feminist strength, self-expression, and resilience. Her vibrant self-portraits, imbued with raw emotion and powerful symbolism, continue to captivate audiences worldwide. This enduring fascination has propelled her art into the realm of global cultural iconography, making her presence felt in museums, exhibitions, and popular culture in countless ways.

Museums around the world have dedicated significant space to showcasing Frida Kahlo's art. The Casa Azul, her former home in Coyoacán, Mexico, has been transformed into the Museo Frida Kahlo, a testament to her life and work. This museum houses a substantial collection of her paintings, drawings, personal belongings, and photographs, providing visitors with an intimate glimpse into her life and creative process. Other major museums, including the Museum of Modern Art (MoMA) in New York City, the Tate Modern in London, and the Centre Pompidou in Paris, have also included her works in their permanent collections, further solidifying her place in the global art canon.

Beyond permanent collections, Frida Kahlo's art continues to be the subject of major traveling exhibitions, attracting large crowds and generating widespread media attention. These exhibitions often explore specific themes in her work, such as self-portraiture, surrealism, or her relationship with Diego Rivera. They also feature lesser-known works, giving audiences a deeper understanding of her artistic evolution and creative process. These traveling exhibitions have helped to introduce Frida Kahlo to new audiences worldwide, cementing her status as a global artistic icon.

Frida Kahlo's influence extends beyond the realm of fine art, permeating popular culture in diverse ways. Her distinctive style, characterized by vibrant colors, bold imagery, and a powerful feminine presence, has inspired countless artists, musicians, designers, and fashion houses. Her iconic unibrow and flower-adorned hair have become instantly recognizable symbols of her personality and style. Her art has been featured in films, television shows, music videos, and countless other forms of media, further solidifying her place in the public consciousness.

Frida Kahlo's iconic imagery has been appropriated by numerous brands, designers, and artists for commercial purposes. From clothing and accessories to furniture and home decor, her art has been reinterpreted and reimagined to appeal to a broad audience. While this commercialization has raised concerns about the potential for cultural appropriation, it also speaks to the enduring popularity and cultural relevance of her work. Her art has become a source of inspiration for a new generation of artists and consumers, demonstrating the lasting impact of her uniquely powerful artistic voice.

The ubiquitous presence of Frida Kahlo's art in museums, exhibitions, and popular culture is a testament to her enduring legacy. Her powerful self-portraits, imbued with personal struggles and feminist themes, have resonated with audiences across generations and cultures, solidifying her place as a global cultural icon and a symbol of artistic resilience and self-expression. Her legacy continues to inspire and empower, reminding us of the transformative power of art and the importance of embracing our individuality.

Her influence on artists, musicians, and designers around the world

Frida Kahlo's influence transcends the boundaries of time and geography, resonating deeply with artists, musicians, and designers across the globe. Her vibrant, often painful, and unapologetically authentic self-portraits have served as a powerful source of inspiration for generations of creative minds, leaving an indelible mark on artistic expression.

For artists, Kahlo's work has become a veritable wellspring of inspiration, particularly for those navigating themes of identity, pain, and resilience. Her fearless embrace of her physical and emotional struggles, often depicted with unflinching honesty, empowers artists to explore their own experiences with vulnerability and strength. Her use of vivid colors, symbolic imagery, and surrealist elements has influenced a diverse range of artistic styles, from contemporary painting and photography to mixed media installations and performance art.

Contemporary artists like Cindy Sherman, who utilizes self-portraits as a means to explore gender identity and social constructs, and Jenny Saville, whose large-scale figurative paintings delve into the complexities of the female body, owe a debt to Kahlo's pioneering approach to self-representation. Artists like Frida Kahlo, with her unique artistic vision, challenge traditional artistic norms, paving the way for future generations of artists to express themselves freely and authentically.

In the realm of music, Kahlo's legacy has found expression in diverse genres, from rock to pop to folk. The raw emotionality and unflinching honesty of her work have resonated deeply with musicians seeking to capture the complexities of the human experience. Her powerful imagery and enduring spirit have fueled countless musical interpretations, with artists drawing inspiration from her life, struggles, and artistic vision.

Musicians like Florence Welch of Florence + The Machine, whose music often delves into themes of identity, vulnerability, and strength, have cited Kahlo as a key influence. Singer-songwriter Lana Del Rey, whose haunting and evocative lyrics explore themes of love, loss, and the complexities of the feminine, has also drawn inspiration from Kahlo's work. The enduring legacy of Frida Kahlo's artistic vision has found a powerful voice in contemporary music, influencing artists to explore personal narratives and delve into the depths of human emotion.

Beyond the realms of fine art and music, Kahlo's influence extends to the world of fashion and design, inspiring a wide range of creative expressions. Her vibrant and eclectic style, characterized by bold colors, traditional Mexican attire, and a bold use of accessories, has become a defining element of global fashion trends. Her unibrow, her signature floral headbands, and her vibrant use of color have been embraced by designers, stylists, and fashion icons worldwide, transforming her into a timeless fashion icon.

High-end designers like Jean Paul Gaultier, whose work often incorporates elements of Mexican culture and indigenous motifs, have paid tribute to Kahlo's legacy. Fashion houses like Gucci and Valentino have incorporated Kahlo-inspired elements into their collections, reflecting the enduring influence of her style. The vibrant colors, intricate details, and bold spirit of Kahlo's fashion sense continue to inspire designers to create clothing that celebrates individuality and embraces cultural diversity.

Frida Kahlo's impact on artists, musicians, and designers extends far beyond mere inspiration. Her unwavering spirit of self-expression, her unflinching exploration of pain and vulnerability, and her celebration of cultural heritage have served as a powerful catalyst for creative expression. Her artistic vision continues to resonate with creative minds across the globe, reminding them that authenticity, resilience, and individuality are the cornerstones of a truly impactful legacy.

Chapter 16: The Frida Kahlo Museum:

The history of the Blue House and its transformation into a museum

The Blue House, a vibrant and historic dwelling in Coyoacán, Mexico City, served as both the home and artistic sanctuary of the legendary painter Frida Kahlo. This iconic structure, painted in a striking shade of cobalt blue, has witnessed the unfolding of Kahlo's life, love, and artistic evolution, becoming an integral part of her legacy. Now known as the Frida Kahlo Museum, the Blue House stands as a poignant testament to her enduring spirit and artistic genius.

The Blue House, originally named Casa Azul, was built in the late 19th century by Kahlo's father, Guillermo Kahlo, a photographer of German origin. The house, with its distinctive blue exterior, became a symbol of Kahlo's early life, filled with memories of her childhood and the formative years that shaped her artistic sensibility. The house also held a special significance for Kahlo as a place where she could escape from the outside world, finding solace and inspiration in her art.

The Blue House witnessed the tumultuous love story of Kahlo and the renowned muralist Diego Rivera. They married in 1929 and resided in the Blue House for a significant period, making it a hub for their artistic endeavors and social gatherings. The house played host to renowned artists, intellectuals, and revolutionaries, becoming a focal point for artistic discourse and political activism. The walls of the Blue House echoed with conversations about art, politics, and the future of Mexico.

However, the Blue House also bore witness to the complexities and challenges of their relationship. The passionate love story of Kahlo and Rivera was marked by infidelity and emotional turmoil, which found expression in Kahlo's art. The house became a canvas for her artistic struggles, her pain, and her resilience. The vibrant colors and bold symbolism of her paintings, often inspired by the surroundings of the Blue House, reflected her inner world and the tumultuous emotions she carried.

After Kahlo's death in 1954, the Blue House remained mostly untouched. In 1958, Rivera donated the house and its contents to the Mexican government with the intention of preserving Kahlo's legacy. The Blue House was meticulously preserved, showcasing the life and work of the artist in a manner that would honor her memory and artistic contributions.

The Blue House officially opened as the Frida Kahlo Museum in 1986, becoming a pilgrimage site for art enthusiasts and admirers of Kahlo's art. The museum houses a remarkable collection of Kahlo's paintings, drawings, and personal belongings, offering visitors a glimpse into her life, struggles, and artistic process. The museum also features a collection of photographs, letters, and other artifacts, providing further insight into the artist's personality and artistic evolution.

The Frida Kahlo Museum, a vibrant blue haven amidst the bustling streets of Coyoacán, stands as a testament to the enduring legacy of Frida Kahlo. It serves as a place where visitors can immerse themselves in the world of the artist, exploring her art, her life, and her struggles. The museum's vibrant colors, symbolic imagery, and intimate details reflect the spirit and artistic vision of one of the most iconic artists of the 20th century. The Blue House, transformed into a museum, continues to inspire generations, reminding us of the power of art to transcend pain, celebrate resilience, and celebrate the power of the human spirit.

Preservation of her legacy and artistic heritage

Frida Kahlo's legacy extends far beyond her captivating self-portraits and the tumultuous life she lived. It encompasses a powerful message of resilience, self-expression, and the enduring power of art to transcend personal struggles and inspire generations. The preservation of her artistic heritage has become a crucial endeavor, ensuring that her work and its profound impact continue to resonate with audiences around the world.

The **Blue House**, the iconic building in **Coyoacán**, Mexico City, where Frida Kahlo was born and lived for much of her life, has been transformed into the **Frida Kahlo Museum**. This museum serves as a vital repository of her artistic legacy, showcasing her paintings, personal belongings, and the intimate spaces that shaped her life and artistic vision. It stands as a testament to her enduring influence, inviting visitors to delve into the complexities of her life and the profound messages embedded in her art.

The museum's dedication to preserving Frida Kahlo's legacy extends beyond simply displaying her works. It actively promotes research and scholarship on her life and art, providing a platform for scholars, curators, and art enthusiasts to explore the nuances of her artistic practice and its broader significance. The museum's curatorial team meticulously preserves her paintings, ensuring their long-term preservation through advanced conservation techniques. This meticulous approach ensures that future generations can continue to experience the raw power and emotional depth of her artwork.

The **Frida Kahlo Museum** also plays a crucial role in promoting cultural exchange and education. It hosts exhibitions, workshops, and educational programs, encouraging a deeper understanding of Frida Kahlo's life and art. These initiatives are designed to reach audiences of all ages, fostering a sense of appreciation for her artistic vision and its enduring influence. The museum's website and social media platforms further amplify her legacy, making her art accessible to a global audience and fostering a vibrant community of admirers.

Beyond the walls of the museum, the preservation of Frida Kahlo's legacy is a collaborative effort. Art historians, curators, and museums around the world dedicate themselves to studying, exhibiting, and promoting her work. The continuous circulation of her paintings through exhibitions and retrospectives keeps her legacy alive, ensuring that her artistic vision remains relevant and inspiring to contemporary audiences.

The ongoing efforts to preserve Frida Kahlo's legacy reflect the profound impact her art has had on the world. Her paintings continue to captivate audiences, sparking conversations about identity, gender, pain, and the human condition. The preservation of her artistic heritage ensures that her voice, powerful and unflinching, will continue to resonate for generations to come, leaving an enduring mark on art, culture, and feminist discourse.

The museum's role in showcasing her life and work to the world

The Casa Azul, or Blue House, in Coyoacán, Mexico, was more than just Frida Kahlo's home; it was a crucible of creativity, a sanctuary of pain and passion, and a testament to her indomitable spirit. After Kahlo's death in 1954, the house, which had served as a haven for her art, her life, and her love for Diego Rivera, was transformed into a museum, a permanent testament to her extraordinary legacy. This act of preservation not only enshrined her artistic brilliance but also served as a vital conduit for bringing her life and work to a global audience.

The Frida Kahlo Museum, as it is formally known, opened its doors to the public in 1958, becoming a pilgrimage site for art enthusiasts and admirers of Kahlo's unique spirit. It houses a treasure trove of her personal belongings, including paintings, sketches, photographs, letters, and clothing, providing a captivating glimpse into her world. The museum's collection offers a comprehensive portrait of

Kahlo, capturing her physical and emotional landscapes, her artistic evolution, and her enduring struggle against adversity. Visitors are transported through time, witnessing the evolution of her artistic style, the intricate symbolism woven into her self-portraits, and the profound influence of her Mexican heritage.

The Casa Azul itself serves as a backdrop to her life story. The vibrant blue walls, adorned with vibrant murals and filled with the spirit of Kahlo's artistic vision, become a canvas for visitors to imagine her life within those walls. Her studio, where she battled pain and poured her soul onto canvas, is preserved as a shrine to her creative process, allowing visitors to feel a sense of connection to the artist's intimate world. The museum's curator, Hilda Trujillo, has dedicated her career to preserving the authenticity of the space, ensuring that it remains a testament to Kahlo's spirit and creative energy.

The museum's role extends beyond simply displaying Kahlo's artwork. It actively engages with audiences, fostering a deeper understanding of her life, her work, and her place in history. Through curated exhibitions, lectures, workshops, and educational programs, the museum aims to educate visitors about Kahlo's artistic process, her political convictions, her personal struggles, and her lasting impact on the world. It provides a platform for scholars, artists, and students to explore the complexities of Kahlo's art and life, sparking dialogue and critical thinking about her enduring legacy.

The Frida Kahlo Museum is not merely a repository of art; it is a vibrant space that celebrates her life and work. It provides a platform for visitors to engage with her art on a personal level, to connect with her spirit, and to find inspiration in her resilience. The museum's impact transcends geographical boundaries, making Kahlo's story accessible to a global audience, ensuring that her artistic vision and her powerful message of self-expression continue to resonate for generations to come.

Chapter 17: Frida Kahlo's Continuing Influence:

The ongoing relevance of her art and messages in contemporary society

Frida Kahlo's legacy transcends time, resonating deeply with contemporary audiences in ways that continue to inspire, challenge, and provoke. Her art, a potent blend of personal pain, cultural identity, and revolutionary spirit, speaks to a range of issues that remain undeniably relevant in the 21st century, from the complexities of identity and self-expression to the fight for equality and the exploration of the human condition.

One of the most enduring aspects of Kahlo's work is its unflinching portrayal of pain and suffering. Through her iconic self-portraits, she confronts the viewer with the raw reality of her physical and emotional struggles, inviting us to grapple with the complexities of human vulnerability. In a world often obsessed with idealized beauty and the pursuit of perfection, Kahlo's honesty and courage in presenting her own imperfections serve as a powerful reminder that suffering is a shared human experience, and that embracing our fragility can be a source of strength and resilience.

Kahlo's art also speaks directly to the ongoing struggles for gender equality and self-determination. Her depictions of female sexuality, often challenging societal norms and traditional expectations, have made her a powerful feminist icon. She challenged the objectification of women, celebrated female strength and autonomy, and explored the complexities of female identity in a way that continues to resonate with a growing movement for female empowerment.

Beyond gender, Kahlo's art serves as a potent commentary on the broader human experience. Her exploration of the body, both its beauty and its fragility, speaks to the interconnectedness of our physical and emotional selves. She challenges us to consider the power of the body as a vessel for both pain and pleasure, a site of both vulnerability and resilience. This exploration of the body remains relevant in a world that often feels conflicted about its own physicality, struggling with societal pressures and evolving definitions of beauty.

Kahlo's artistic style itself is a testament to her defiant spirit and unique vision. Her embrace of surrealism allowed her to blend reality and fantasy, creating dreamlike worlds that reflected her own inner landscapes. Her vivid colors, bold imagery, and symbolic details invite viewers to actively engage with her art, to decipher its layers of meaning and uncover the personal narratives that lie beneath the surface.

Furthermore, Kahlo's art serves as a powerful reminder of the importance of cultural identity and the need to celebrate our own roots. She embraces her Mexican heritage, incorporating traditional clothing, textiles, and imagery into her work, showcasing the richness and beauty of her cultural background. This celebration of cultural heritage remains relevant in a world increasingly defined by globalization and the potential homogenization of culture.

In conclusion, Frida Kahlo's art continues to resonate with contemporary audiences due to its unflinching exploration of pain, its celebration of female empowerment, its exploration of the human body and its limitations, its embrace of surrealism, and its celebration of cultural identity. Her legacy transcends time, serving as a powerful reminder of the enduring power of art to confront societal norms, explore the complexities of the human experience, and inspire a sense of individual empowerment and self-acceptance.

The exploration of themes such as body image, identity, and self-acceptance

Frida Kahlo's life was a tapestry woven with threads of pain, resilience, and a profound exploration of the human condition. Beyond the vibrant colors and surrealist imagery of her paintings, lies a deeper narrative – one that grapples with themes of body image, identity, and self-acceptance.

Throughout her life, Frida battled with chronic pain and physical limitations, a consequence of a devastating bus accident that left her with lifelong injuries. Her art became a canvas for confronting these challenges, a means of reclaiming her own narrative and forging a unique sense of self amidst adversity. Her self-portraits, often stark and unflinching in their depiction of her physical struggles, served as potent statements of self-affirmation and a refusal to be defined by her physical limitations. Her body became a symbol of resilience and strength, an instrument of resistance against the societal expectations that sought to confine her.

Kahlo's art didn't shy away from revealing the vulnerability of the human form. Her paintings often featured stark anatomical details, including blood, wounds, and medical instruments, confronting the viewer with the raw reality of her physical experiences. This was not a display of despair, but rather a defiant assertion of selfhood. By choosing to paint her own pain, Frida reclaimed agency over her body and its narrative.

Identity is a recurring theme throughout Kahlo's work. Her self-portraits, often rendered in bold and vibrant colors, served as a visual exploration of her own evolving identity. She experimented with various guises, incorporating traditional Mexican attire, symbols of her indigenous heritage, and even the occasional unibrow, a defining feature that challenged conventional beauty standards. Frida was not afraid to be different; she embraced her individuality and challenged the prevailing notions of femininity.

Beyond the physical, Frida's art delved into the complexities of self-acceptance. The pain she endured, both physical and emotional, became a catalyst for introspection. Her art became a means of confronting her own demons, of navigating the turbulence of her relationships, and of embracing the multifaceted nature of her identity.

In her paintings, Frida challenged societal norms and expectations. She rejected the idealized feminine image and celebrated the strength and resilience of the female spirit. Her art embodied a spirit of defiance, a refusal to be confined by societal expectations. It was a powerful message of self-empowerment, urging viewers to embrace their own individuality and navigate the world with authenticity and conviction.

Frida Kahlo's art served as a beacon of hope and inspiration for countless individuals. Her unflinching self-portraits, her bold use of color, and her powerful exploration of themes such as body image, identity, and self-acceptance, continue to resonate with viewers across generations. Through her art, she offered a potent reminder of the beauty and strength that lies within each individual's unique journey of self-discovery.

Her lasting impact on art, fashion, and popular culture

Frida Kahlo's influence extends far beyond the canvas, radiating through the corridors of art, fashion, and popular culture, making her a true global icon. Her legacy is not merely confined to her artistic output, but permeates various aspects of contemporary society, serving as a potent symbol of feminist defiance, cultural pride, and the enduring power of the human spirit.

In the realm of art, Frida Kahlo's impact is undeniable. Her unique style, a vibrant blend of surrealism and Mexican folk art, has inspired countless artists and movements. Her self-portraits, imbued with intense introspection and raw emotion, became a defining feature of her work, inspiring artists to explore their own identities and experiences with greater depth and vulnerability. Her iconic use of bold colors, symbolic imagery, and the fusion of reality and dreams continues to resonate in contemporary art, challenging traditional notions of beauty and representation.

Beyond the visual arts, Frida Kahlo's influence has seeped into the world of fashion. Her signature unibrow, bold lips, and intricate floral headbands have become cultural touchstones, inspiring designers and fashion houses to embrace bold individuality and celebrate the beauty of unconventional styles. Her love of traditional Mexican clothing, particularly the vibrant Tehuana dress, has inspired countless designers to incorporate Mexican textiles and motifs into their collections, highlighting the rich cultural heritage of Mexico and celebrating the power of cultural expression.

Frida Kahlo's presence extends far beyond the art galleries and fashion runways, penetrating the fabric of popular culture. Her image, often rendered in vibrant colors and dramatic angles, graces everything from t-shirts and tote bags to tattoos and murals, becoming a ubiquitous symbol of feminist empowerment and artistic rebellion. She has been the subject of numerous films, documentaries, and books, further solidifying her status as a cultural icon. Her life and work have inspired musicians, writers, and filmmakers, further amplifying her message of self-acceptance, resilience, and the celebration of individuality.

Frida Kahlo's enduring legacy lies in her ability to inspire and resonate with people from all walks of life. Her art transcends borders, cultures, and generations, serving as a reminder of the power of self-expression, cultural pride, and the human spirit's capacity to overcome adversity. Her influence continues to shape and inspire the artistic, fashion, and cultural landscape, ensuring that her story and her art will continue to captivate and inspire generations to come.

Chapter 18: The Enduring Legacy:

Reflecting on Frida Kahlo's legacy and her enduring influence

Frida Kahlo, the iconic Mexican painter, transcended the boundaries of art and became a symbol of resilience, self-expression, and feminist empowerment. Her life, marked by physical pain, emotional turmoil, and a relentless pursuit of artistic truth, has resonated with generations, leaving an indelible mark on art, culture, and the global consciousness.

Kahlo's legacy is not simply about her vibrant and symbolic paintings, but about the spirit that permeated her art and life. She defied societal expectations, embraced her pain and vulnerabilities, and used her art as a powerful tool for self-discovery and social commentary. Her self-portraits, often depicting her physical and emotional struggles, became a powerful reflection of the female experience and a challenge to the traditional portrayal of women in art.

Her enduring influence is evident in the countless ways she continues to inspire:

1. A Feminist Icon:

Kahlo's defiance of gender roles, her celebration of female strength and sexuality, and her outspokenness against societal expectations made her a powerful figure for the feminist movement. She challenged the patriarchal norms of her time, and her work continues to resonate with feminists around the world, offering a poignant reminder of the ongoing fight for equality and self-determination.

2. A Symbol of Resilience:

Kahlo's life was riddled with pain and adversity. She endured a debilitating bus accident, multiple surgeries, and ongoing physical and emotional struggles. Yet, she refused to be defined by her suffering. Instead, she channeled her pain into her art, transforming it into a powerful expression of resilience, strength, and the indomitable human spirit. Her story inspires those facing their own challenges to find strength within themselves and to embrace their vulnerabilities as sources of power.

3. An Artistic Visionary:

Kahlo's art transcended stylistic boundaries. While often categorized as Surrealist, she developed her own unique visual language, blending elements of realism, symbolism, and personal mythology. Her work is characterized by vivid imagery, bold colors, and a raw emotional honesty that continues to captivate and inspire artists, art critics, and art lovers alike. Her influence can be seen in the work of contemporary artists who explore themes of identity, self-expression, and the human condition.

4. A Cultural Icon:

Kahlo's image, with her signature unibrow, vibrant clothing, and iconic flowers, has permeated popular culture. She has become a symbol of Mexican identity and a global icon, celebrated in music, fashion, literature, and film. Her work has been adapted for contemporary audiences, reinterpreted in various forms, and continues to resonate with a diverse global audience.

Frida Kahlo's legacy is a testament to the transformative power of art. She used her brush to confront her own pain, celebrate her identity, and challenge societal norms. Her life and work continue to inspire us to embrace our individuality, face our challenges with resilience, and use our voices to create change in the world.

Her story is a powerful reminder that art can be a force for healing, self-expression, and social commentary. It is a testament to the enduring power of the human spirit and the impact that a single individual can have on the world.

Her impact on art, feminism, and Mexican culture

Frida Kahlo's life and art have left an indelible mark on the world, transcending the realm of mere artistic brilliance to become a potent symbol of resilience, self-expression, and feminist ideals. Her impact reverberates across the domains of art, feminism, and Mexican culture, leaving a legacy that continues to inspire and empower generations.

A Revolution in Art:

Frida Kahlo's artistic vision challenged the conventions of her time, paving the way for a new wave of artistic expression. Her self-portraits, often raw and unflinchingly honest, delved into the depths of her personal struggles, from physical pain to emotional turmoil. This raw, unfiltered approach to art resonated with audiences, who saw themselves reflected in her vulnerability and strength. She defied the traditional depiction of women in art, refusing to be defined by societal expectations. Instead, she painted her own narrative, a powerful testament to the complexities of female experience.

Her art defied categorization, weaving together elements of Surrealism, Mexican folk art, and personal symbolism. This unique blend of styles created a powerful and distinctive visual language, one that resonated with the burgeoning feminist movement of the time. Her bold use of color, her embrace of the grotesque and the beautiful, and her unflinching portrayal of her own body, particularly its imperfections, all contributed to a powerful sense of liberation, challenging the traditional norms of beauty and femininity.

Frida's influence on the art world is undeniable. She inspired countless artists to embrace self-expression, to confront uncomfortable truths, and to create art that is deeply personal and socially relevant. Her art became a touchstone for the emerging feminist movement, offering a powerful visual representation of female strength, resilience, and the complex reality of women's lives. Her enduring influence continues to be felt today, as artists continue to draw inspiration from her boldness, her vulnerability, and her unwavering commitment to authenticity.

A Feminist Icon:

While Frida Kahlo never explicitly identified as a feminist, her life and work resonated deeply with the growing feminist movement. Her defiance of societal expectations, her embrace of her own sexuality, and her celebration of the female body, all stood as powerful symbols of female agency and self-determination. She challenged traditional gender roles, refusing to be confined by the expectations placed upon women in a patriarchal society.

Her self-portraits, particularly those featuring strong, independent women, resonated with feminists, offering a visual representation of female power and self-worth. She became a symbol of female resilience, a woman who endured pain and suffering, but ultimately triumphed through her art. Frida's life story, marked by physical and emotional challenges, became a powerful testament to the strength and spirit of women, inspiring countless women to embrace their own identities and to fight for equality.

Her image, with its distinctive unibrow, colorful clothing, and fierce gaze, became a powerful symbol of feminist activism. She inspired women to embrace their own unique beauty, to challenge traditional norms, and to fight for their rights. Her legacy continues to be celebrated by feminists worldwide, who recognize her as a trailblazing figure in the fight for gender equality and female empowerment.

A Cultural Ambassador:

Frida Kahlo's connection to Mexican culture was deeply ingrained in her art, making her a powerful ambassador for Mexican heritage and identity. Her paintings celebrated Mexican folklore, traditions, and indigenous culture, weaving together vibrant colors, symbolic imagery, and themes of national pride. She integrated Mexican clothing, textiles, and flora into her self-portraits, showcasing the richness and beauty of her cultural heritage.

Her work became a bridge between the modern and the traditional, blending European Surrealism with the ancient traditions and folklore of Mexico. She introduced the world to the vibrant spirit of Mexican culture, its rich history, and its enduring traditions. Her work became a powerful symbol of Mexican identity, both within Mexico and around the world.

Frida Kahlo's legacy continues to be celebrated in Mexico. Her iconic image adorns murals, textiles, and souvenirs, a testament to her enduring popularity and her role as a cultural icon. The Frida Kahlo Museum, housed in her former home, "The Blue House," attracts millions of visitors each year, eager to experience her art and to connect with the vibrant spirit of Mexican culture that she so passionately embodied.

In conclusion, Frida Kahlo's impact on art, feminism, and Mexican culture is immeasurable. She transformed the art world, inspiring a new wave of self-expression and authenticity. Her work became a powerful symbol of female resilience and self-determination, a testament to the strength and spirit of women. She became an ambassador for Mexican culture, celebrating its richness and beauty on a global stage. Her legacy continues to inspire generations, reminding us of the power of art to challenge conventions, to celebrate diversity, and to inspire change.

The continuation of her story and her ongoing relevance in the 21st century.

Frida Kahlo's story doesn't end with her physical departure in 1954. Her legacy, much like her art, has transcended time and space, resonating with audiences across generations and cultures. As we navigate the complexities of the 21st century, Frida's message of **self-expression**, **resilience**, and **embracing one's authentic self** remains as potent as ever.

Her art, once confined to the walls of the **Blue House** in Coyoacán, has become a global phenomenon, gracing museums, galleries, and the homes of art enthusiasts worldwide. Her iconic **self-portraits**, filled with vivid imagery and raw emotion, continue to captivate viewers, inviting them to delve into the complexities of her life and her artistic vision.

Frida's enduring appeal lies in her ability to connect with a diverse audience on a personal level. Her struggles with **pain**, **illness**, and **physical limitations** resonate with individuals facing their own challenges, reminding them of the power of the human spirit to persevere. Her **celebration of womanhood** and her defiance of societal norms continue to inspire countless women and individuals who identify with her unwavering spirit of **independence**.

Beyond her artistic contributions, Frida's influence extends to the realms of fashion, popular culture, and even politics. Her unique **style** – characterized by vibrant colors, traditional Mexican attire, and her signature unibrow – has become a symbol of individuality and self-expression. Her image adorns clothing, accessories, and countless other products, reminding us that **beauty** can be found in embracing our uniqueness.

Frida's legacy is not simply about her art; it's about her **life** as a whole. It's about the woman who defied expectations, embraced her pain, and used her art as a powerful tool for **self-expression** and **social commentary**. She remains an enduring symbol of **feminist** ideals, reminding us that we have the power to define our own narratives, challenge societal norms, and embrace our individuality.

In the 21st century, where individuality is increasingly celebrated, Frida Kahlo's story continues to resonate deeply. She serves as a powerful reminder that art is not simply about aesthetics; it's about **expression**, **connection**, and the power of the human spirit to overcome adversity. Her legacy inspires us to embrace our **authentic selves**, to find beauty in our **flaws**, and to use our voices to create positive change in the world.

Printed in Great Britain
by Amazon